The 1840s

The Victorian Society
Studies in Victorian architecture and design

Volume One

The 1840s

Edited by Rosemary Hill
and Michael Hall

THE VICTORIAN SOCIETY

London · 2008

The Victorian Society is the champion for Victorian and Edwardian architecture and related arts in England and Wales. Lectures, walks and tours are organised for members, who also receive this journal and *The Victorian,* our thrice-yearly magazine. For information contact: The Victorian Society, 1 Priory Gardens, London W4 1TT.

www.victoriansociety.org.uk .

The publication of this first volume of *Studies in Victorian architecture and design* has been made possible by a generous bequest from Dorothy Cathilda Fraser, for many years a member of the Victorian Society, and is dedicated to her memory.

ISBN 978-0-901657-50-3
ISSN 1756-6460

Designed and typeset in Kepler by Dalrymple
Printed by Nicholson & Bass, Belfast

Frontispiece: The study, Sandon Hall, Staffordshire. Photo: *Country Life* Picture Library. See Paul Bradley's article on pp.30–41.

The 1840s

STUDIES IN VICTORIAN ARCHITECTURE AND DESIGN · VOLUME 1

Introduction: Architecture and the 1840s

ROSEMARY HILL

In this first issue of 'Studies in Victorian architecture and design' we begin at the beginning with essays on aspects of architecture in the first full decade of the reign. What follows is a brief overview of the period and of the buildings and ideas that chiefly characterised it.

On April 27, 1840 the corner stone of the New Palace of Westminster was laid by Sarah Barry, Charles Barry's wife. It was a modest, not to say furtive, ceremony, an oddly muffled note on which to begin the most prominent public building of the decade. The element of embarrassment was due no doubt to the fact that Barry had promised in 1836 that the Palace would be all but finished in four years, in fact it had taken that time to put the foundations in. Controversy dogged the building throughout the 1840s and its changing fortunes in the press and public opinion tell in microcosm the story of the decade. The debates that surrounded it, about the nature and purpose of public art, the role of the architect and of the decorator, the proper style for the age, were those that dominated architecture as a whole while the debates that took place within it, in the temporary chambers of the Lords and Commons, on the repeal of the corn laws, the Maynooth grant and the papal aggression, charted the social and religious upheavals through which the Victorian age and its architecture emerged.

The first full decade of Victoria's reign was one of extreme contrasts. The 'hungry forties' were marked by poverty and civil unrest: the strikes and riots of 1842, the famine in Ireland, the railway boom and crash and, in 1848, a succession of revolutions across Europe. Yet it was also a time of excitement and hope. The last of the Georgian age – corruption in public life and decadence in private – had it seemed been swept away. The twenty-one-year-old Queen had replaced the last of her wicked uncles, William IV, and youth was in the ascendant. Those who were later to be eminent Victorians were still young, with most of their best work ahead of them. George Eliot and Ruskin were in their twenties; Gladstone, Darwin, Tennyson and Livingstone in their thirties. Even Carlyle was only forty-five. If the 'condition of England' question was on every thoughtful person's mind, then there was no shortage of energetic voices offering an answer. Across Europe there were movements variously known as Young England, Young Ireland and Young Italy. Perhaps it was not until the 1960s that another decade had its tone so much determined by the rising generation.

Fig. 1 | St Giles, Camberwell, London, by George Gilbert Scott, 1842–44

This was true in architecture too. If we remember the 1840s principally as the age of A.W.N. Pugin and the Gothic revival that is not so much because the Gothic was yet the dominant style – it was a notably eclectic decade – nor because Gothic buildings were always the best – Pugin's own work was very mixed in its success – it is because the Goths and their admirers were young, vocal and closely engaged with the issues of the day. Pugin himself was twenty-eight in 1840. His followers, who went on to become the leading architects of the High Victorian period, George Gilbert Scott (1811–78), William Butterfield (1814–1900), G. E. Street (1824–81) and J L Pearson (1817–97), all made their names as young men while their most influential admirers and critics, the sternly discriminating ecclesiologists Benjamin Webb, John Mason Neale and Alexander Beresford Hope were in their twenties too. Between them they brought about not only a new phase of the Gothic Revival, more scholarly and more 'real' – to use their favourite term of praise – than the Georgian, they introduced a different idea of what architecture should be, what Scott described as 'a truer sense of the dignity of the subject'. [1]

The young architects of the 1840s were political and philosophical, none more so than Pugin, who, like Webb, Neale and Hope, was a Romantic Tory. For them, the answer to the condition of England question was a return to an older order, a benign, Catholic (but not necessarily Roman Catholic), hierarchy in which the interests of land and aristocracy were preserved against the growing forces of trade, radicalism and the city. The problem of the modern, industrial city, 'a system of life constructed on a wholly new principle' in which social and moral order had to be recreated anew, was to haunt the Victorian age.[2] As the decade began Pugin addressed it directly in a revised edition of his manifesto *Contrasts*, published in 1841. It contained the plates that are now among the most famous examples of Victorian social criticism, the contrasted towns of 1440 and 1840 and 'Contrasted Residences for the Poor' [Fig. 2]. Not everyone could agree with Pugin's personal credo, that Gothic architecture was the only true style for a Christian country, but nobody could deny that in comparing the panopticon with the medieval monastery he was comparing like with like. Each was the built expression of a particular view of the human condition: the Utilitarian and the Catholic. It was a fair point and a topical one at a moment when opposition was mounting to the New Poor Law, which forced people into the workhouse, where families were split up and living conditions often bestial.

These images, which were soon followed by Pugin's *True Principles* and an article in the *Dublin Review*, illustrating his designs for churches, excited Scott, 'almost to fury'.[3] Having begun his career with workhouses and sadly 'incorrect' churches he was not alone in experiencing a sense of being 'morally awakened' as the new decade began.[4] His first important church, St Giles, Camberwell [Fig.1], opened in 1844 and much influenced by Pugin, marked a new departure. It was, as Scott himself immodestly said, 'the best church by far that had then been erected'; at least it was the best Gothic church and only Gothic churches mattered

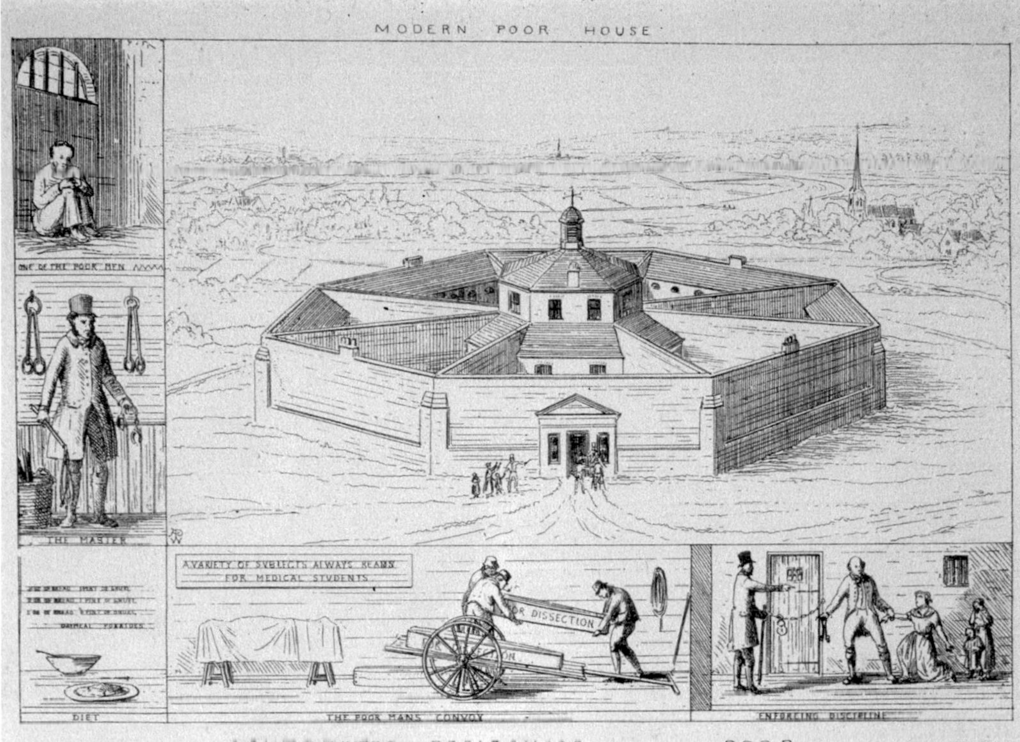

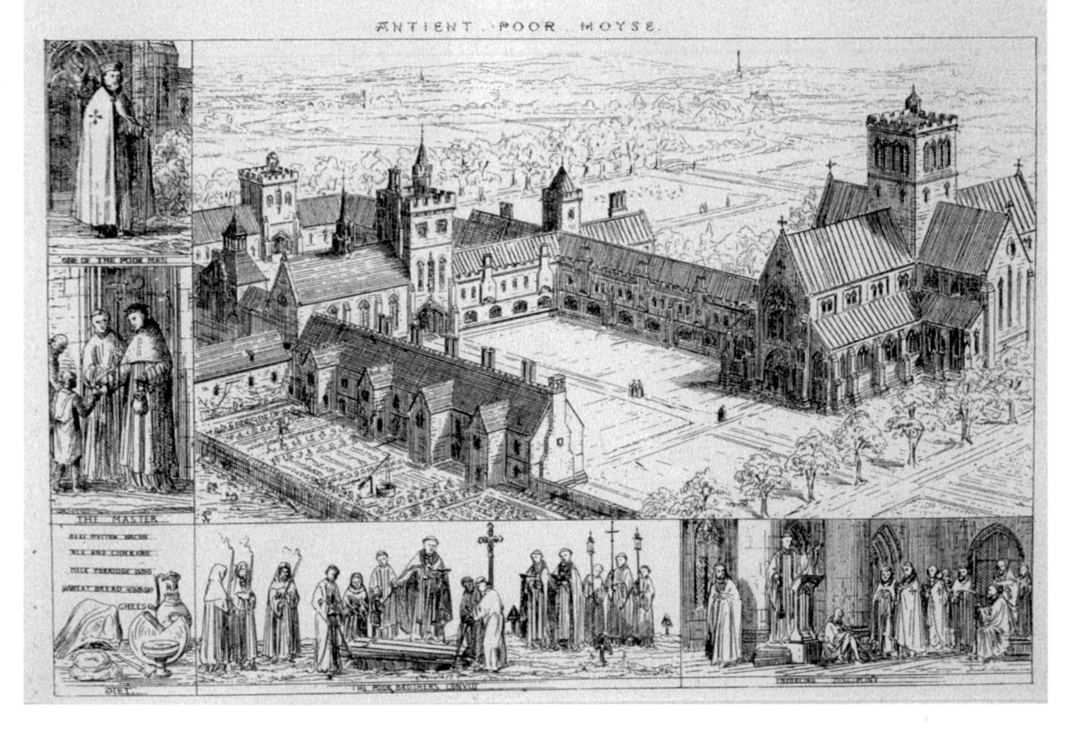

Fig. 2 | 'Contrasted Residences for the Poor', from *Contrasts*, by A. W. N. Pugin, second edition, 1841

Fig. 3 | *A View of Trafalgar Square* by Charles Deane (fl. 1815–55), after 1843, oil on board

Fig. 3 | The Ashmolean Museum and Taylorian Institution, Oxford, by C. R. Cockerell, 1841–45

to the rising generation.[5] Not surprisingly there were few attempts to realise in full Pugin's vision of Ancient Charity. Pugin himself built St John's Hospital at Alton in Staffordshire for Lord Shrewsbury and Salvin's client at Peckforton in Cheshire, Lord Tollemache, who was 'of the generation of the Young Englanders', built cottages for all his workers, in the belief that 'to witness the improvement in [their] social condition' was the only real purpose of being a landowner.[6] More generally however it was by the building of churches and the creation of parishes that a solution was sought. As Pugin put it, 'It is by parish churches that the faith of a nation is to be sustained and nourished.'[7] In the towns, new churches were often accompanied by schools and other buildings for communal use, especially where there was a wealthy private patron such as Angela Burdett Coutts for whom Benjamin Ferrey built St Stephen, Rochester Row, in 1847–50 [Fig. 5]. In the countryside the idea of the group of rural buildings, church, houses and school as an ideal Christian community, was also born in the 1840s, in Pugin's buildings at Ramsgate and Butterfield's at Coalpit Heath, Gloucestershire [Fig. 6], though it was to mature only in the next decade.

It was the Gothic church that emerged as the first and arguably the greatest Victorian building type. St Giles, Camberwell, marked the fullest expression so far of the Puginian ideal; 14th-century English, symmetrical, aisled and spired, the model with which Pugin, according to Webb and Neale, first brought 'the thing required into *Reality*'.[8] It was a type that reached its apogee in Pugin's own St Giles, Cheadle, opened in 1846, by which time it was already slightly past its meridian. The energetic young Goths had soon exhausted its potential. Street's St Mary's Par, Cornwall of 1847, Pugin's St Marie, Rugby (1848), and Butterfield's Cumbrae College (1844–9; Fig. 7] all showed them experimenting with a tougher more sculptural and eclectic style that came to be known as High Victorian.

But what a church looked like in the 1840s was only half the point. Even its effectiveness as a purveyor of social order and justice was secondary to its essential meaning. It was what it symbolised of Christian faith and human experience that mattered to the opinion formers of the 1840s, especially the members of the Cambridge Camden Society. The CCS, which rapidly transformed itself in the early years of the decade from a small undergraduate body to a force in national life, dictated the principles of 'ecclesiology' to bishops and architects alike. Although there was much insistence on ecclesiology being a science, it was as much mystical as empirical. 'We would allege', wrote Webb and Neale, in their introduction to the works of Durandus, 'that everything material is symbolical of some mental process, of which it is indeed only the development: that we may see in everything outward and visible some inward and spiritual meaning. It is this which makes "books in everything"'.[9]

Deep chancels, rood screens, which stand 'between two worlds, the one immoveable the other changeful', the correct forms of piscinas, the position of fonts, these were the direct expressions of faith, they argued, so true that to interfere or misinterpret them was to tinker with the Word of God.[10] It was a peculiarly early

Fig. 5 | *left* St Stephen, Rochester Row, London, by Benjamin Ferrey, 1847–50

Fig. 6 | *above* The vicarage, Coalpit Heath, Gloucestershire, by William Butterfield, 1845

Fig. 7 | *below* Cumbrae College by William Butterfield, 1844–49

Fig. 8 | St George's Hall, Liverpool, designed by James Elmes, 1840–41, completed by C. R. Cockerell and Sir Robert Rawlinson, 1847–56

Victorian kind of mysticism, spiritual but checkable, a steam-age metaphysics suited to an age equally in thrall to past and future, romance and 'reality'. It had a great appeal not only to young architects but to all of their contemporaries through whom the Oxford Movement had already sent out 'the vibration of an intellectual movement', towards church reform.[11] The eager members of the CCS, equipped with their forms and 'orientators' (for finding true East) surveyed old churches and criticised new ones with a will.

For all of which the Gothic Revival was not, as the essays elsewhere in this volume make clear, the whole story of early Victorian architecture. While the Palace of Westminster continued to rise and Barry's strictly symmetrical Perpendicular looked more and more unsatisfactory to the ecclesiologists, it remained almost unique as a public building in the Gothic style. Although Gothic banks, town halls and university buildings would come later, nearly all the major civic buildings of the 1840s and most of the new railway stations were classical. The Greek Revival had faded fast, it was Roman and Renaissance classicism that inspired James Bunning's Coal Exchange (1847–49) and William Tite's Royal Exchange (1842–44) as well as two of the finest classical buildings of the century, James Elmes's St George's Hall, Liverpool (designed 1840–41), and Cockerell's Ashmolean Museum, Oxford (1841–5). Elmes, however, died young while Cockerell, like Barry, the other great classical architect of the decade, belonged to an older generation.

One of Barry's major buildings of the 1840s was Bridgewater House (1847–50) in London. It makes a revealing contrast to the Palace of Westminster, for while the Palace spoke of a new Victorian age, Bridgewater House, one of the last great private mansions to be built in the capital, belonged already, as a building type, to an earlier era. The days of the aristocratic urban palace were numbered. In secular architecture the young Victorians' contribution was in the creation of quite a different sort of domestic idiom, intended for the middle-classes to meet the demand for 'the smaller detached houses which the present state of society has generated'. [12] They invented the sort of substantial, suburban home made possible by the railways, which allowed the professional classes to live at a distance from their place of work. Pugin's houses, at Ramsgate, Rampisham in Dorset and Childwall near Liverpool, with their central staircase living halls, combining the plan of the Regency villa with that of the medieval manor, set the example to Butterfield at Coalpit Heath.[13] It was one of the most original but least acknowledged contributions of the 1840s, a legacy that Shaw and Nesfield later developed into what would become eventually Hermann Muthesius's typical *Englische Haus.*

The country house, meanwhile, was not much touched by the latest architectural thinking. Only at the end of the decade, after the House of Lords was opened in 1847, would the modern Gothic or Palace of Westminster style become fashionable. The great houses of the 1840s were mostly built for comfort and, unlike the Georgians', privacy. Country-house visiting declined sharply from the beginning of the decade while a growing emphasis on family life, from the monarchy downwards, reduced the number of public rooms a country house required. Victoria and Albert's Osborne House (1845–51) was designed by Thomas Cubitt and Albert himself in an Italianate style to be above all 'convenient' and 'spacious'.[14] In many cases style was a question left up to the client while the expertise of the architect, notably the ever-busy William Burn, was chiefly seen to lie in planning, which became more complex over the years. The grand enfilade was replaced by individual reception rooms within which the separate spheres of family, servants, children and guests were required to be kept apart. Then there was the all-important dinner route to be devised.

Fig. 9 | Mr Pecksniff (right), first and nastiest of fictional architects, from Charles Dickens's *Martin Chuzzlewit* (1843)

What architecture should be – Christian, Gothic and moral, according to the young – was one question that dominated the decade. Another was the status of the architect himself. The 1840s was the decade in which the profession became organised. Distinctions between amateurs and professionals, between builders, surveyors and designers, began to be drawn more clearly and rigidly. By 1843 architecture had already become 'too much a profession' for the high-minded Webb and Neale.[15] The Institute of British Architects received its royal charter in 1837; the Architectural Association was founded in 1847 and the architect became for the first time a distinct figure in the public imagination. January 1843 saw the appearance of Dickens's Mr Pecksniff, the first and probably the nastiest architect in modern fiction, whose social pretensions were matched only by his professional dishonesty. One of his more unpleasant characteristics was his tendency to plagiarise his pupils' work and this too, the question of authorship in architecture, was one that interested the 1840s. As with so much, the test case was the Palace of Westminster. It was the competition for the palace that seems to have given rise to the short-lived phrase 'Art-Architect', intended to distinguish a building's designer from those who merely carried it out, and as Pugin became more famous rumours that he was the real art-architect circulated widely, especially among the young. He was not, but the troubled experience of the palace, a building of 'unprecedented scale and complication' that shortened the life of both its designers made further specialisation inevitable.[16]

With professional institutions and specialisation came journals. Architecture was more widely discussed and illustrated in the 1840s than ever before. The *Builder* was founded in 1842 and became the mouthpiece of the profession. Other periodicals came and went. John Weale, the antiquary and publisher, was responsible for several short-lived but interesting ventures, including Weale's *Quarterly Architectural Papers*. William Leeds, whose career had begun in the 1830s on Loudon's magazine, was perhaps the first architectural critic in the modern sense. A prolific author and a brilliant linguist, able to put his readers in touch with the latest European and Scandinavian developments, Leeds was no admirer of the Gothic Revival and had several heated exchanges with Pugin in the *Civil Engineer and Architect's Journal*. He also, however, attacked Cockerell, as Professor at the Royal Academy, for refusing to teach Gothic. The time had come, he and others felt, to challenge the Academy's dictatorship. It was another parting of the generations. Beyond the still-small specialist press contributors to the *British Critic*, *Fraser's Magazine* (where Leeds also published) the Liberal Catholic *Rambler* and the *Ecclesiologist* all wrote, often caustically, about architecture. The *Ecclesiologist* was particularly merciless, sounding often like a jaded prep-school master: 'The architect rejoices in the name of Gribbon', it complained, of a new Presbyterian church in Dublin; 'we were astonished at the audacity of its badness.'[17] The Oxford Architectural Society was just as dogmatic in its publications, if less sarcastic. It was no wonder George Wightwick complained that 'In this age when everybody must meddle with his neighbour's business ... no set of persons have suffered more, from the interference and dictation of their neighbours than the architects. It seems ...that any body who has read Rickman, or Aunt Elinor, is qualified to criticise.'[18] But the critics' taste, if not their tone, has been largely vindicated. The architects they took seriously have stood the test of time, while the Gribbons are not much lamented.

The tremendous energy that ushered in the 1840s and saw architecture rise to new heights of moral and social ambition had reached its peak by the middle of the decade. In 1845, after a series of violent internal quarrels, the CCS changed its name to the Ecclesiological Society and moved to London. It continued to exert a considerable influence, but its heyday had passed. This was also the year of Newman's conversion and with his departure and that of many of his circle to Rome, some of the creative tension went out of the religious debate. The ideal of reunion between Roman and English Catholics became an impossibly distant prospect, although some, like Pugin, clung to it. The romantic Tories who had called themselves Young England were divided over the vote for the Maynooth grant – to fund the expansion of the Catholic college and seminary near Dublin – and that movement too began to fragment. The young Victorians were growing up and going their separate ways. The raw enthusiasm of 1841 gave way to a more thoughtful and pragmatic mood, not least because the regeneration of architecture was turning out to be more complicated than had been at first foreseen. Looking back from the 1860s, Leeds's obituarist Henry Hyde recalled the enthusiasts of the 1840s and their naïvety: 'the young and rising men of the day ... thought they should have an early harvest, but everything had to be fresh created ... whole trades had perished, and had to be restored ... Free plasterers work, carving and panelling, had become almost extinct.'[19]

By the end of the decade the truth of Hyde's observation was already apparent: the reform of design and the architectural crafts was becoming a matter of urgent concern. The Government School of Design was generally considered a failure. A Royal Commission was set up to oversee the decoration of the Palace of Westminster, the interiors of which were intended to display the finest arts and crafts of the age, but competitions to undertake the work produced poor results. Wood and stone carving were largely lost arts while stained glass, one of the most elusive techniques but one of the most necessary for Gothic, continued to baffle a handful of pioneers. Only Pugin, who began work for Barry at the Palace in 1844, had managed to assemble anything like a team of skilled craftsmen in all the necessary media. Meanwhile, manufactured goods multiplied in quantity but not in aesthetic quality. In 1849 two men set out to tackle the problem, from diametrically opposite points of view. Henry Cole, the utilitarian, launched his *Journal of Design* and with it the campaign for design reform, and John Ruskin published *The Seven Lamps of Architecture*, an appeal to the spirit as much as the practice of craftsmanship. Cole thought Ruskin a dreamer with a 'very lopsided view of railways',[20] to which Ruskin replied, mildly enough, 'that a man can only write effectively when he writes from conviction'.[21] However, both men, although they disagreed on means, had the same end in view and both were immensely influential. They were confident of achieving reform on a grand scale and their confidence was better founded than Pugin's had been in 1841.

Perhaps the new decade truly began in May 1851, when the strains of the Alleluia Chorus rose through the Crystal Palace. In the 1850s the nation became self-consciously Victorian. The word itself was coined and the mood of the country was optimistic. There was still poverty. The over-crowded cities were still a source of anxiety, but overall as Britain emerged onto the world stage as a great imperial power its prosperity was felt to increase. The religious agonies of the 1840s were for most Anglicans over. The Gorham Judgement had seen a great exodus to Rome of the most active High Church clergy, leaving the field clear, for a while at least, for the Protestant Broad Church of Prince Albert. A more muscular age, for architecture and for Christianity, was dawning. Pugin was in the grip of his last illness. His admirers Scott and Butterfield were becoming established as gentlemen architects with offices and clerks, which Pugin had never countenanced. The Palace of Westminster was still, of course unfinished, but All Saints, Margaret Street, the Ecclesiologists' show church was just beginning. Most of the masterpieces of Victorian architecture were still in the future, there was plenty to look forward to, but the 19th century would not recapture the febrile excitement of these early years: 'never glad confident morning again'.[22]

NOTES

1. Gavin Stamp (ed.), *Personal and Professional Recollections by Sir George Gilbert Scott*, Stamford, 1995, p. 87.
2. Asa Briggs, *Victorian Cities*, London, 1990, p. 12.
3. Stamp, op. cit. [note 1 above], p. 88.
4. Ibid.
5. Ibid., p. 92.
6. Quoted in Mark Girouard, *The Victorian Country House*, New Haven and London, 1979, p. 156.
7. A.W.N. Pugin, *The Present State of Ecclesiastical Architecture in England*, London, 1843, p. 1. The book reprints two articles by Pugin published in the *Dublin Review*.
8. John Mason Neale and Benjamin Webb (eds), *The Symbolism of Churches and Church Ornament, a translation of the first book of the Rationale Divinorum Officiorum, written by William Durandus sometime Bishop of Mende*, Leeds, 1845, p. xix.
9. Ibid., p. li.
10. Ibid. (quoting Thiers), p. lxxiii.
11. George Eliot, 'Amos Barton', in *Scenes of Clerical Life*, 3rd edition, London, 1860, vol. 1, p. 46.
12. A. W. N. Pugin, *An Apology for the Revival of Christian Architecture*, London, 1843, p. 38.
13. See Rosemary Hill, 'Pugin's Small Houses', *Architectural History*, vol. 41 (2003), pp. 147–74. and, for the link with Butterfield, Rosemary Hill, 'Pugin's Churches', *Architectural History*, vol. 44 (2006), pp. 179–205.
14. Queen Victoria, quoted in Jill Franklin, *The Gentleman's Country House and its Plan*, London, 1981, p. 240.
15. Neale and Webb, op. cit. [note 8 above], p. xxi.
16. Andrew Saint, *The Image of the Architect*, New Haven and London, 1983, p. 61.
17. 'Architectural Room of the Royal Academy' *The Ecclesiologist*, vol. 9 (1849), p. 371.
18. George Wightwick, 'Publications of the Oxford Architectural Society', in *Weales Quarterly Papers on Architecture*, vol. 4, London, 1845, p. 1. *Aunt Elinor's Lectures on Architecture*, published anonymously in 1843, was the work of Mary Holmes, a friend of Newman who later became governess to Pugin's children. It was a hugely popular work of genteel ecclesiology dedicated to 'the ladies of London'.
19. Hyde Clark, 'William Henry Leeds, Architectural Critic', *Building News*, October 11, 1867, p. 697.
20. *Journal of Design*, October 1849, p. 72.
21. Quoted in Michael W. Brooks, *John Ruskin and Victorian Architecture*, London, 1989, p. 99.
22. Robert Browning, 'The Lost Leader', in *Dramatic Romances and Lyrics*, London, 1845, The phrase is often quoted but is perhaps uniquely evocative of the moment when it was published, in the middle of the first Victorian decade.

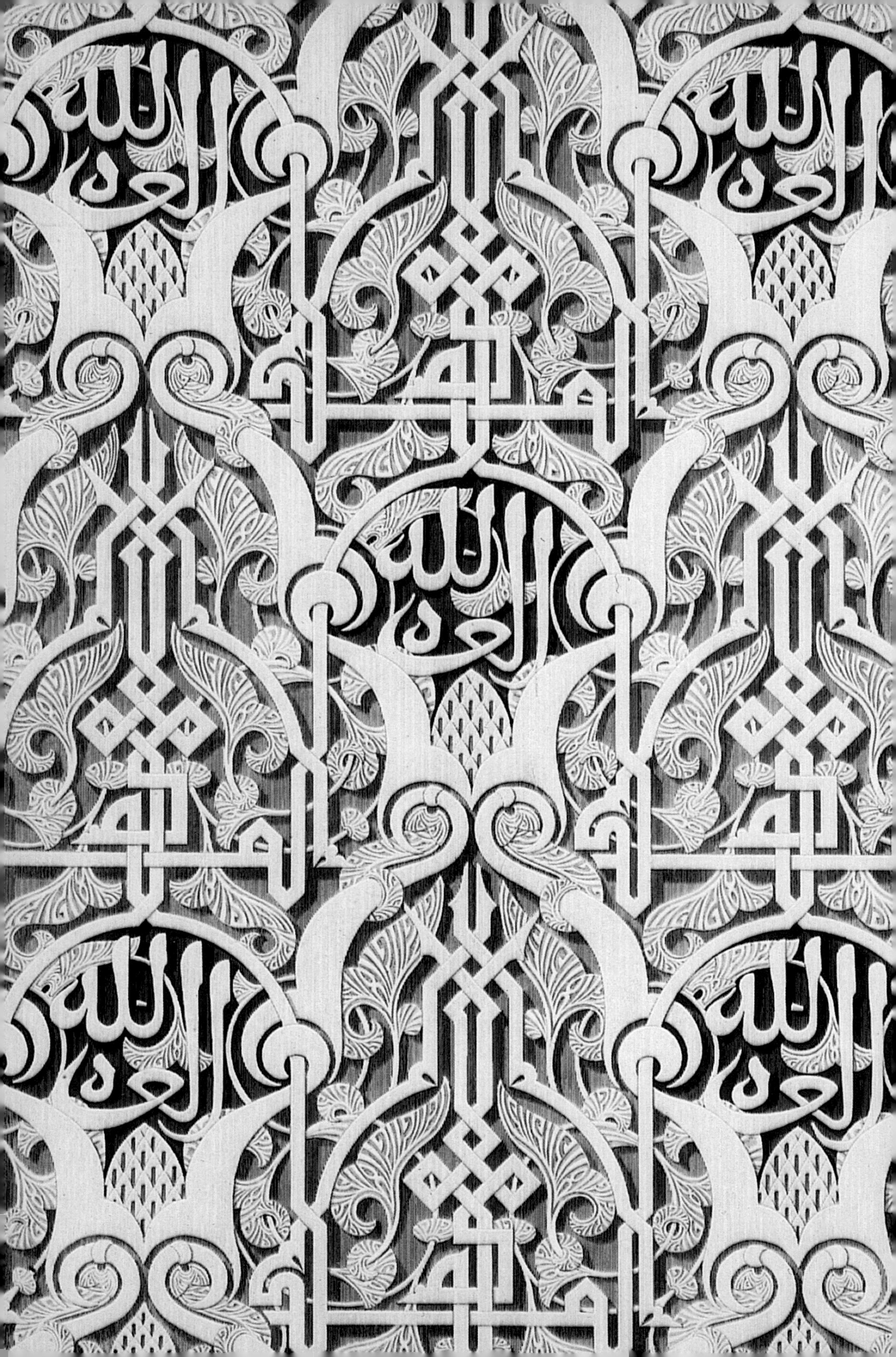

1 · From gilded dream to learning laboratory: Owen Jones's study of the Alhambra

CAROL A. HRVOL FLORES

One of the most famous and lavish publications of the 19th century, Owen Jones's 'Alhambra' is more often celebrated than studied. Here it is considered as architectural history and in its context as part of architectural education in the 1840s.

When the British architect Owen Jones (1809–1874) and the French architect Jules Goury (1803–1834) began their study of the Alhambra in 1834, the 'red castle' in Grenada was a romantic symbol of 'sensuous exoticism' and 'barbaric magnificence'. The imagery of the palace as an 'earthly paradise' had become familiar through the popular writings of Washington Irving and Victor Hugo.[1] By contrast, Jones and Goury undertook a serious investigation of the architecture of the Moors in the 13th and 14th centuries. Their investigation was halted in August 1834, when Goury died from cholera. Jones returned his friend's body to France and then went on to London to publish their findings as *Plans, Elevations, Sections, and Details of the Alhambra* (1836–42, 1842–45).[2] Scholars have discussed the text in relation to Jones's interest in the Middle East and as a milestone in the history of publishing, but here it will be considered in terms of its value to the understanding of architecture and in the context of British architectural education.

Although the practice of architecture changed considerably during the first decades of the 19th century, the education of British architects made little progress. Most prospective architects continued to be articled to practitioners for a period of five to seven years. Students supplemented this uneven and unregulated training with optional drawing classes, lectures at the Royal Academy and periods of foreign travel.[3] Although the need to improve this system was identified in the founding objectives of the Architectural Association (1831) and the Institute of British Architects (1834), concerns over fees for service, unscrupulous competitions and the deterioration of craftsmanship took precedence over educational reform. Resources for study were also limited. With the exception of works by Vitruvius, Palladio and Serlio, few treatises had been translated into

Figure 1 | Detail of ornament, Owen Jones, *Plans, Elevations, Sections, and Details of the Alhambra*

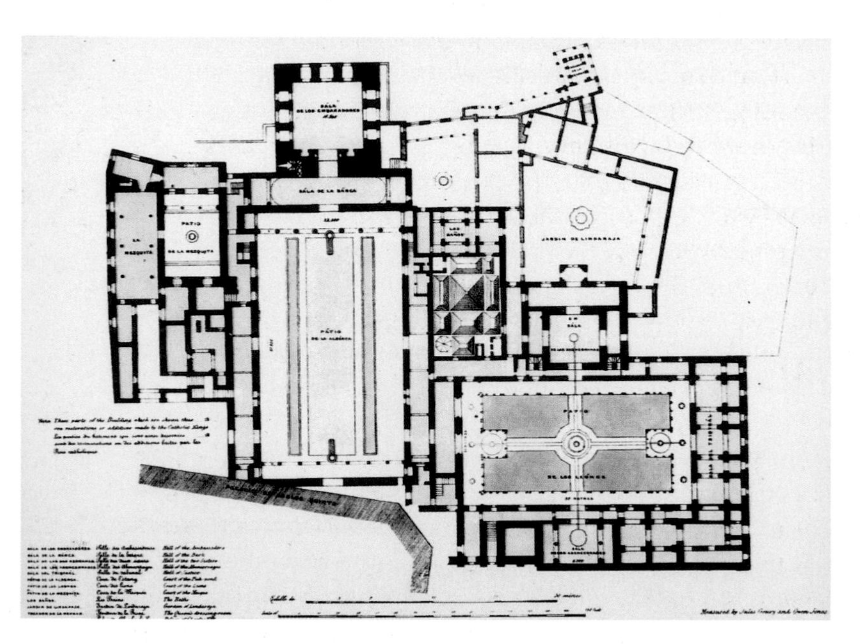

Fig. 2 | General Plan of the Fortress of the Alhambra, Owen Jones, *Plans, Elevations, Sections, and Details of the Alhambra*, Plate I, Volume I

Fig. 3 | Plan, Comares Palace and the Lion Court Palace, Owen Jones, *Plans, Elevations, Sections, and Details of the Alhambra*, Plate II, Volume I

Fig. 4 | Section, Patio of the Lions, Owen Jones, *Plans, Elevations, Sections, and Details of the Alhambra*, Plate XV, Volume I

English and contemporary works by British authors lacked theoretical insights and critical analysis.[4] Although antiquarian authors speculated on the origin and nomenclature of Gothic architecture, most of the English texts consisted of illustrations of picturesque villas and cottages or the architecture of particular places.[5] The study of construction, materials and aesthetics produced by Jones introduced new standards for architectural research and reporting.

Jones dedicated the *Alhambra* to Goury and recognised him as coauthor. He also prefaced the text with a quotation from Victor Hugo's *Les Orientales* (1829) and a history of the palace written by the noted Arabic scholar Pascual de Gayangos (1809–97). The decision to include the history is significant for two reasons: first, as evidence of Jones's serious commitment to scholarship, and second, as proof of his conviction that a society's beliefs are reflected in its architecture. To develop this understanding further, Jones commissioned Gayangos to translate the epigraphs covering every surface of the Alhambra to reveal the thoughts and feelings of its patrons and designers [Fig. 1].[6] Although these translations and the history by Gayangos were important, the substance and main contribution of the text was the graphic representation and analysis of the palace's architecture by Jones and Goury. Their findings were presented in two volumes: the first includes text and illustrations and the second contains enlarged details from the earlier plates. Information is conveyed in text and through a variety of graphic techniques, from simple sketches and measured plans to sections and highly complex renderings.

The first wood-block print presents a distant view of the Spanish acropolis [Fig. 2]. The Alhambra is not shown from a particular vantage point, but as a composite of several perspectives based upon accurate depictions of the buildings. The use of the composite enabled Jones to provide an introduction to the various buildings comprising the Alhambra in one image.[7] Each plate throughout the text provides a wealth of information. Some plates establish comparative studies of an architectural element, such as column capitals, spandrels or decorative panels, by illustrating several examples. Each piece shows the characteristics and components of the element and the ensemble illustrates the stylistic variations [Fig. 6]. Other plates combine plans, elevations, profiles and details of a particular space on one page [Fig. 7]. The renderings [Fig. 5] are comprehensive drawings of spaces within the Alhambra. These images were unprecedented in both size and the amount of detail. The accuracy of the information and the precision of the depictions still draw the attention and approval of scholars.[8]

Measured plans [Fig. 3] indicate the natural and man-made elements at the site and the chronology of the buildings. The accompanying texts describe the original purpose of spaces and structures as well as their contemporary functions. In this way, the reader learns that the ancient citadel is now used to house prisoners and that the houses, gardens and convent situated in the 'Calle San Francisco' and the 'Alhambra Alta' occupy the area of the former mosque and the house of the Cadi. Jones explains that the architecture of the Moors mirrored their religious beliefs. He supports this hypothesis with examples depicting the influence of Islamic practices and symbolism on built form, including the purpose of *mihrabs* and the dual functions of lattice windows, which admit light into the upper corridors and offer the harem screened views of the feasts below.[9] Jones's study of the palace's construction corrected earlier misconceptions and revealed new information to explain the mysteries of the complex.[10] For example, he ascertained that the *muqarnas,* or stalactite domes, that intrigued and mystified western visitors, consisted of wooden ceilings that appeared to be supported by pendentives made of reed and plaster. Jones observed that the stalactite dome in the Hall of the Sisters contained almost 5,000 of these plaster prisms, arranged mathematically, and noted that the prisms derived from seven forms based on the right-angle triangle, the isosceles triangle and the rectangle. The straight surfaces and angle of the curves allowed the prisms to be combined in complex arrangements. This explanation of the *muqarnas* is typical of Jones's method of providing data, identifying the mathematical and physical basis of the construction, while recognising the 'wonderful power and effect obtained by the repetition of the most simple elements.'[11] Other components, such as column capitals, spandrels, and arches, receive the same type of examination [Fig. 8].[12]

Jones differentiated between modern and original materials and used his first-hand knowledge of Islamic architecture to speculate upon and reconstruct missing elements (Fig. 9). For example, he noted the aesthetic disparity between the extant brick and marble floors and the palace's tile decoration. He also observed that the patterns of many mosaics were obscured at the lowest level, indicating that the floors had been raised or that the existing materials had been installed on top of earlier foundations. Since Jones believed that the Arabs created unified aesthetic arrangements, he attributed the incongruous selection of materials and raised floors to the remodelling efforts of later Christian inhabitants. Jones marvelled at the durability and intense colours of the tiles and studied their manufacture. He learned to differentiate *azulejos* from tessellated tiles. *Azulejos* are made from earthenware clay covered with white slip, painted and fired, while tessellated tiles are formed by pressing wet clay into moulds, impressing patterns into the clay, then filling the impressions with coloured liquid and firing.[13] His interest was both historical and contemporary. He described the Arabs' methods of producing tiles and discussed the contemporary experiments by Pether and Singer in England to adapt the manufacture of tiles to machine production. Jones took samples of the Arabic tiles to Minton, Blashfield and other English manufacturers to assist in their experiments with the revival of tile production.[14]

Jones also discovered that the Arabs' profuse geometrical motifs and two-dimensional patterns were derived from two basic grids.[15] The first grid was formed from equidistant horizontal and perpendicular lines crossed diagonally on each square and the second involved diagonal lines intersecting in each alternate square. Jones recognized the potential offered by the grids for an infinite number of patterns achieved by changing the colours of the ground, the surface lines, or both. Each change altered the balance, highlighting different elements and producing interlaces, stars and other motifs. This discovery of a rational basis to design influenced his promotion of two-dimensional geometric and conventionalised patterns over the florid realism popular at the time. Jones also analysed ornament in terms of perception. He explained that at a distance, the eye identifies the outline of forms and masses, and discerns details only upon closer inspection.[16] In the same way, he discussed perception in regard to colour, asserting that at a distance, compositions of balanced primary colours produce a lively 'bloom', while secondary and tertiary colours dissipate into lifeless shadow. Jones observed that the Moors used the primary colours (blue, red and yellow,

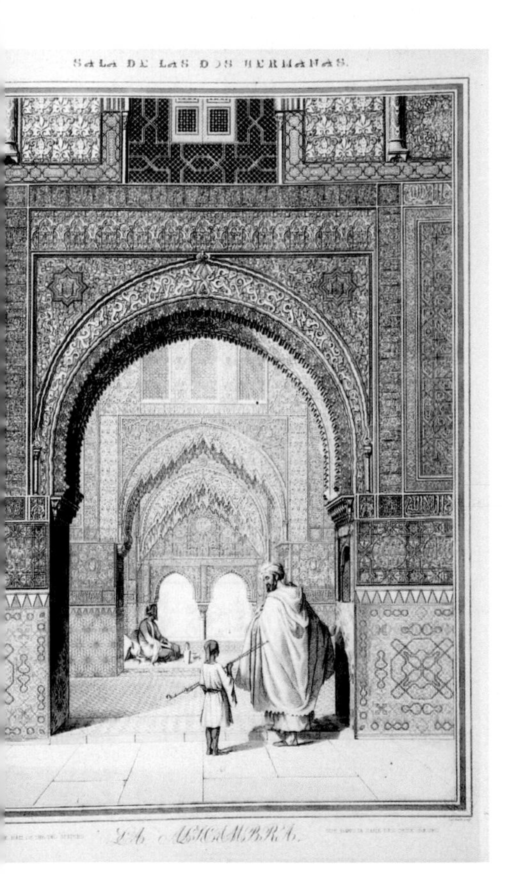

Figure 5 | View from the Hall of the Two Sisters to the belvedere of the Linderaja, Owen Jones, *Plans, Elevations, Sections, and Details of the Alhambra*, Plate XIX, Volume I

Figure 6 | Lintels, Owen Jones, *Plans, Elevations, Sections, and Details of the Alhambra,* Plate XXXV, Volume II

Figure 7 | Plan, Elevations, Section, Detail, The Mosque, Owen Jones, *Plans, Elevations, Sections, and Details of the Alhambra*, Plate XXV, Volume I

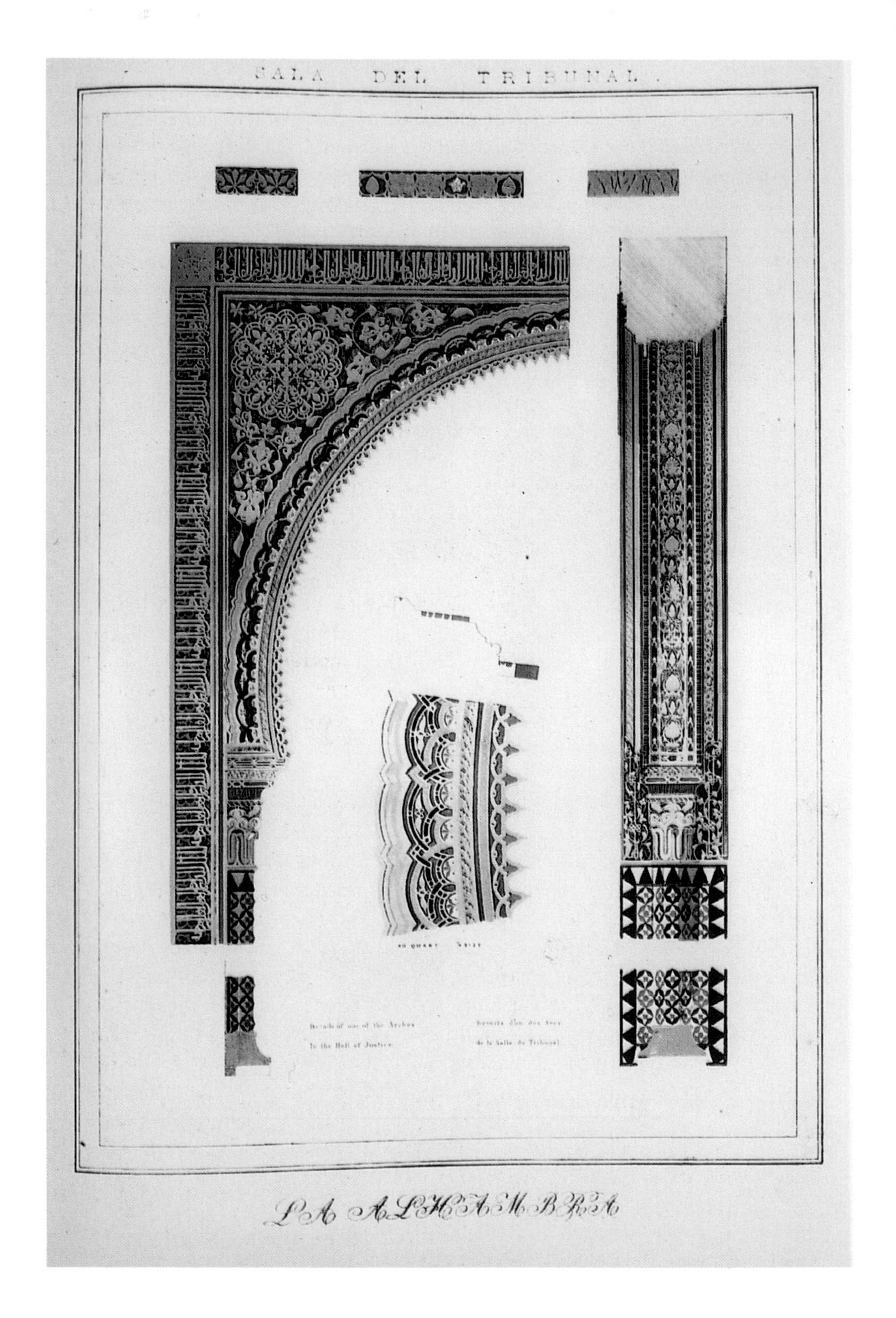

Figure 8 | Details of an Arch, Hall of Justice, Owen Jones, *Plans, Elevations, Sections, and Details of the Alhambra*, Plate XXVII, Volume I

or gold) on ceilings and the upper surfaces of walls and placed the secondary colours (purple, green, and orange) lower to provide relief from the brilliant colouring above. He offered two explanations for the prevalence of green grounds evident in much of the extant decoration. The first suggested that the green resulted from the original metallic blue ornament changing in colour over time, a proposal supported by particles of blue pigment still observable in crevices throughout the palace. The second possibility attributed the choice of green to later restorers. Jones said their work was easily identified by the coarseness of the execution and the imbalanced colours chosen in contrast to the harmonious schemes of the Moors.

The study of colour in ancient architecture was the source of considerable debate in the 19th century and was probably the motive for Jones and Goury's selection of the Alhambra for their research. They had studied colour in architecture throughout the Middle East and a study of the colours used in the oldest surviving medieval palace in Europe promised to be a worthwhile contribution to the debate on polychromy. Jones explains his position in terms corresponding to Aristotle's argument about the decline of art, maintaining that the Arabs, Egyptians and Greeks used primary colours during periods of high art, while secondary colours were dominant in periods of decline.[17] Fragments of red and blue pigments and gilding remained on column capitals in the Alhambra, but the shafts showed no traces of colour. Jones speculated that the shafts had been gilded in harmony with the capitals, but the gold was removed during restorations to eliminate the expense of re-gilding.[18] This hypothesis parallels Hittorff's contention that the Greeks had developed a system of polychromy as refined as their system of form and, thereby, a trained eye could assess the accuracy of a colour scheme based on the degree of harmony.

Before Jones and Goury's investigation of the Alhambra, Arabic architecture had been dismissed as insubstantial and lacking in originality, beyond the development of kiosks, fountains and *caravanserai*. Jones and Goury's detailed study of the construction, materials, ornament and colour in the Spanish palace challenged this assumption and bestowed the same respect and consideration on Islamic architecture as had previously been reserved for Greek, Roman and Renaissance structures. Even more significantly, their study introduced a new level and model of scholarship appropriate to future architectural inquiries.

The *Alhambra* also introduced another boon to education and publication, the use of colour printing to provide reliable and detailed information. Illustrations in colour had been almost inaccessible since each printed image had to be tinted by hand, a slow, expensive, inconsistent process. Although experiments in colour printing had been conducted with some success in France, Germany, and England, no London publisher was capable of printing the number of plates in multiple colours that Jones desired. Undaunted, the determined young architect purchased presses, hired assistants and after considerable experimentation and frustration, produced the remarkable chromolithographic plates in bold, gouache-like primaries depicting the original and contemporary colours in the Moors' palace.[19]

Plans, Elevations, Sections and Details of the Alhambra won immediate acclaim for the beauty and technical achievement of the colour printing and for being a practical work of utmost value to the profession. Critics called it 'the most perfectly illustrated architectural work' they had ever seen and Joseph Gwilt listed it in the 1842 edition of *The Encyclopedia of Architecture* as an essential study for every student and practitioner.[20] In France, Volumes V and VI (1844 and 1845) of the *Revue Generale [accents] de l'Architecture*, a journal that proclaimed itself dedicated to 'detailed presentations of the studies and experience of eminent men in architecture' and 'surpassing all other periodicals in the deep and serious examination of many important questions,' devoted 27 pages to Jones's text, including over 25 illustrations, excerpts, and a comprehensive summary prepared by the editor, Cesar Daly. Daly praised Jones's scholarship and endorsed his theories and analysis.

Jones produced chromolithographic plates for other architectural studies, including his own *Designs for Mosaic and Tessellated Pavements* (1842), *Encaustic Tiles* (1843) and *Views on the Nile* (1842). He also produced title pages and plates for the works of others, including Henry Gally Knight's *The Ecclesiastical Architecture of Italy* (1842, 1843); Frederick Catherwood's *Views of Ancient Monuments in Central America, Chiapas and Yucatan* (1844); E. Adams's *The Polychromatic Ornament of Italy* (1846) and John Weale's *Quarterly Papers on Architecture* and *Divers Works of the Early Masters in Christian Decoration* (1846). It is interesting to note that the plates in these texts still retain clear and vibrant colours 17 decades after printing and that the *Alhambra* continues to be studied by Islamic scholars and palace restorers.[21]

However, Jones's contributions to architectural education went beyond publication. He donated casts, drawings, and prints from the *Alhambra* to the Architectural Society and sponsored student competitions by offering copies of the *Alhambra* as prizes.[22] He made similar donations to the Architectural Association and to the Institute of British Architects, favouring the Institute with the first copy of the *Alhambra*.[23] He also participated in exhibitions at the Royal Academy and at the Architectural Association.[24] The success of his colour scheme for the Crystal Palace at the Great Exhibition of All Nations in 1851 brought him national attention, affording him the opportunity to present his principles of design in lectures, articles and in *The Grammar of Ornament* (1856). The widespread distribution and adoption of the *Grammar* has overshadowed Jones's extraordinary contributions to the philosophy and study of architecture in the 1830s and 1840s. During the 1830s, he revolutionised architectural thinking in Britain by identifying the correlation between culture and architecture and calling for a new style appropriate to contemporary life and technical capability. In the 1840s, he introduced more precise scholarship and graphics to inform architectural investigation. Although he tried to produce more affordable texts by printing folio

Figure 9 | View, Patio of the Pool (Patio of the Comares), Owen Jones, *Plans, Elevations, Sections, and Details of the Alhambra*, Plate XXXIX, Volume I

and smaller editions and issuing the *Alhambra* in parts to spread the payments, his works were still beyond the means of most students and practitioners. Fortunately, they were still exposed to his books and plates in art and architecture schools in Europe and abroad, where Jones's texts were considered fundamental to the study of design.

Education was critical to Jones's philosophy. Unlike Ruskin, Jones believed that design could be taught and that better education of professionals, manufacturers, and the public was the key to improving British products and taste. He promised students that if they studied the works of the past and the works of nature, and committed themselves to the principles found in both, they could not fail to become creators.[25] His *Alhambra* and other texts assisted their education by expanding the resources for study and improving the level of understanding and presentation of architecture.

NOTES

1. Victor Hugo refers to the Alhambra as the 'Palace that genius / Has gilded like a dream and filled with harmony': *Les Orientales*, Paris, 1829. Washington Irving, *The Alhambra: A Series of Tales and Sketches of the Moors and the Spaniards*, Philadelphia, 1832. For a discussion of the influence of these texts and others as well as the influence of Romantic painters, see John Sweetman, *The Oriental Obsession*, Cambridge, 1987, and Michael Darby, *The Islamic Perspective*, London, 1983.

2. Jones made a brief return visit to Grenada in 1837 to check details.

3. John Wilton-Ely, 'The Rise of the Professional Architect in England', in Sporo Kostof, ed., *The Architect*, New York and Oxford, 1977, p. 197.

4. David Watkin, *The Rise of Architectural History*, London, 1980, p. 64–69.

5. John Archer, *The Literature of British Domestic Architecture 1715–1842*, Cambridge, MA, 1985, p. 23.

6. Carol A. Hrvol Flores, 'Engaging the Mind's Eye: The Use of Inscriptions in the Architecture of Owen Jones and A.W.N. Pugin', *Journal of the Society of Architectural Historians*, vol. 60, no. 2 (June, 2001), pp. 158–167.

7. Antonio Fernandez-Puerta, *The Alhambra: Plans, Elevations, Sections, and Drawings*, London, 1997, vol. 1, p. 161.

8. Marianne Barrucand and Achim Bednorz, *Moorish Architecture in Andalusia*, Cologne, 1992, pp. 10–11; Fernandez-Puerta, op. cit. [note 7 above], p. 88.

9. Mihrabs are discussed in the text accompanying Plate XXV, Volume I, and lattice windows in the text for Plate XIX, Volume I.

10. James Cavanah Murphy's *Arabian Antiquities of Spain*, London, 1813, and *History of the Mahometan Empire in Spain*, London, 1816, were filled with inaccurate information.

11. Text accompanying Plate X, Volume I. Repeated in Albert F. Calvert, *The Alhambra*, London, 1906, p. xliv, and Oleg Grabar, *The Alhambra*, Cambridge, MA, 1978, pp. 178–79.

12. For ceilings [Plates VIII and XVIII], column capitals [XXXIV], spandrels [Plates XXIII, XXXVI], cornices [Plate IX], arches [XXII, XXVII, XXVIII], porticos and pavilions [Plate XIII], windows [Plates IV, XX] and doors [Plate XXXII], all Volume. I; lintels [Plate XXXV, Volume II].

13. Text accompanying Plate XLIV, Volume I.

14. Plate XXXIX, Volume I.

15. Text accompanying Plate XXXVII, Volume I.

16. Text accompanying Plate XXVII.

17. Text accompanying Plate XXXVIII, Volume I.

18. Text accompanying Plate XXXV.

19. Kathryn Ferry, 'Printing the Alhambra: Owen Jones and Chromolithography'. *Architectural History*, vol. 46, 2003, pp. 175–88.

20. *The Athenaeum*, August 4, 1838, p. 556 and August 20, 1842, p. 570. Joseph Gwilt, *The Encyclopaedia of Architecture*, ed. revised by Wyatt Papworth, London, 1867, repr. New York, 1982, p. 1142.

21. Grabar, op. cit. [note 11 above]; Sweetman, op. cit. [note 1 above] and Fernandez-Puerta, op. cit. [note 7 above].

22. Howard Colvin, 'The Architectural Profession', in his *Biographical Dictionary of British Architects 1600–1840*, 4th ed., London, pp. 22–37; *Gentleman's Magazine*, November 3, 1835, December 13, 1836, November 7, 1837, December 5, 1837, and January 5, 1838.

23. Jones gave the copy Number 1 of *Plans ... of the Alhambra* (1836), casts (1838), and various parts of *The ... Alhambra* and two coloured and gilt casts (1839) to the RIBA: Records, Royal Institute of British Architects, London, UK.

24. John Summerson, *The Architectural Association, 1847–1947*, London, 1947, p. 6.

25. Owen Jones, *The Grammar of Ornament*, London, 1868, p. 156.

2 · William Burn and the design (and re-design) of Sandon Hall, Staffordshire

PAUL BRADLEY

A fire in 1848, caused by workmen repairing the roof, robbed the 2nd Earl of Harrowby and his family of their home and propelled them into a lengthy and fraught period of rebuilding.

Sandon Hall in Staffordshire, rebuilt by William Burn, is a rarity. It is one of the few buildings among his prodigious output to remain virtually unaltered and it has stayed in the ownership of the family for whom it was originally built. What makes Sandon's rebuilding compelling is that Burn, an architect with unrivalled experience in designing country houses, struggled to meet the demands of his clients. The developing acrimony was meticulously documented over the troubled seven-year commission and survives as a substantially complete archive.

Burn was born in Edinburgh in 1789, and from the beginning of his extensive practice, in 1814, specialised almost exclusively in providing and altering country houses. He was a versatile and accommodating designer with a reputation for completing commissions on time and to budget. That the 1840s were demanding for Burn and his office is an understatement. Condensed within this period was an output that eclipsed that of any rival and in 1841 it caused Burn to have a breakdown.[1] This was to be only a brief aberration. Granting himself no concessions, once he was back at work commissions were undertaken, completed and replaced as rapidly as ever before. Houses, expertly planned and carefully detailed, of predominantly Jacobethan appearance flowed throughout the decade.[2] An expanding English clientele convinced Burn in 1844 to leave his Edinburgh home and office (and all Scottish projects) in the hands of his partner David Bryce (1803–76), and move to 6 Stratton Street, Piccadilly, in London. The job of rebuilding Sandon Hall for the Earl of Harrowby after a devastating fire in 1848 was precisely the type of commission Burn had hoped would follow his move.

The first person that Lord Harrowby consulted after the fire was the architect-builder Thomas Cubitt (1788–1855), who was engaged to survey the ruin [Fig. 1] and provide proposals for rebuilding. Why Cubitt failed to obtain the commission

Unless otherwise stated, the images illustrating this article have been supplied by courtesy of the Sandon Hall Archive.

Fig. 1 | The sideboard niche in the dining room. Photo: *Country Life* Picture Library

Fig. 2 | *The Ruins of Sandon Hall, June 18*
by an unknown arti

Fig. 2 | The entranc
front, 1905

Fig. 3 | Perspective
view of the entranc
front, May 12, 1852

is not clear, but Burn was a man of enviable political connections, and it was probably this network that persuaded Lord Harrowby, a prominent politician and four times MP for Liverpool, to change his architectural allegiance.[3] With over 130 domestic commissions completed, Burn was an obvious (second) choice.

Sometime around October 1848 Burn made a site visit and proposed that the shell of the main building, and possibly the lower flanking wings, should be reduced to foundation height and a new structure erected upon the footprint. The flanking private wing to the west would be re-roofed and refaced, and retained as part of the new house. The second issue he addressed was style. Burn was a versatile designer whose *oeuvre* included Greek, Tudor Gothic, Jacobethan, Scots Baronial, Italianate and French château styles. Given the consultation of Cubitt and his penchant for Classical-Italianate styling,[4] coupled with the fact that the Countess of Harrowby had spent several years living in Italy, it can be assumed that a house of Italianate appearance had been considered.[5]

Lord Harrowby initiated the discussion about the house's style, out of a concern for cost. If he had been hoping to extract decisive guidance from his architect, he would be disappointed. In a closing paragraph to a letter of December 22, 1848 Burn added a reassuring but non-committal comment: 'I do not conceive there would be any, certainly no material difference of expense between the Tudor and Italian styles.' With no expressed preference, he was happy to place the final decision in the hands of his client. Lord Harrowby took little time reaching a conclusion, and by January 10, 1849 had given Burn sketches of a large Jacobethan edifice, which his son Lord Sandon had prepared. How appreciative the 60-year-old architect felt about receiving stylistic cues from his client's 18-year-old son is not recorded, but the prompt return of the drawings five days later gives an indication. Burn explained 'These sketches I was obliged to take some liberty with, as if fully carried out they would have led to an expenditure much beyond what is contemplated, and I also think to a house considerably too long for the grounds'. So as not to appear ungrateful, he added, 'but the general idea I have in some measure adopted', meaning that his client would get a house of Jacobethan style – the rest would be down to Burn.

Despite being hindered by Cubitt's 'inaccurate' survey drawings, Burn was diligent in sending proposals as early as November 2, 1848, well before Lord Harrowby's letter concerning style or cost. Equally surprising was that he sent not one but three schemes. This was not office practice, and it can be assumed that the question of how much of the old house should be retained was under debate. Plan No. 1 highlighted the negative impact of retaining the wings, as the rebuilt central core became restricted by their existence. In keeping only the private and kitchen accommodation, plans No. 2 and No. 3 offered more fluent arrangements, similar to houses by Burn such as Stoke Rochford Hall, Lincolnshire (1841) and Dartrey, Co. Monaghan (1844), including an entrance front parallel to the garden façade, and a large library occupying the full width of the house. The main staircase would form a physical barrier between the public and private areas, and the south facing principal apartments would be arranged in enfilade, with the sequence following the order in which, most usually, they might be used.

None of the drawings was exactly what the client desired, and on January 10, 1849 plan No. 4 was sent. Principally it was a reworking of the first design, but now retained little of the old house. With this plan came the suggested (and adopted) arrangement of a corridor saloon, with the principal stair to the west, circulation area to the centre and billiard room to the east, with each space demarcated by paired columns. A pencil sketch hurriedly prepared on site proposed that the private and domestic accommodation might extend to the north, creating an 'L' plan entrance forecourt. This was received favourably, and just five days later plan No. 5 was sent in confirmation.[6] Curiously, this latest plan completely reworked the arrangement of the saloon, and repositioned the principal stair, suggesting considerable indecision.

By January 25 Burn was suggesting minor improvements and amendments to the boudoir and immediate area. It is unlikely that he could have anticipated that 10 months later he would be sending a further plan of the principal floor. Although plan No. 2, the last held in the archive and dated November 26, 1849, drew upon previously suggested elements, particularly the saloon / principal stair / billiard room arrangement, the introduction of new motifs such as semi-circular bays and a 'T' plan conservatory, as well as a further reshuffling of the principal rooms to an arrangement differing significantly to what was executed, indicates at least one further revision was instructed. All the component parts that would eventually comprise Sandon as built had now been suggested, albeit spread over five different drawings. Uniting them was proving problematic and a serious drain on office time. Both parties must have begun to be worried. For Burn, it was unprecedented to experience such difficulty in developing a suitable plan: pre-contract revisions were usually trifling adjustments. Similarly, Lord and Lady Harrowby must have been irked that one year after engaging Burn, a plan (the forte of their chosen architect) remained unresolved, and the only elevations they had glimpsed were those by their son.

Little correspondence survives from 1850 and possibly little took place. The lack of new drawings indicates that either the clients were deliberating which of their substantial collection of plans would best suit their needs, or that Burn's attention was focussed elsewhere. A combination of the two is likely, although it is fair to observe that Burn was preoccupied with other equally important commissions as well as with his troubled partnership with David Bryce, which he was about to dissolve.[7] This less than attentive handling prompted Lord Harrowby, when eventually he heard from Burn, to write to Lord Sandon commenting, 'You will be glad to hear of signs of life on the part of Burn.' Yet the Earl and Countess were not so pleased when, on May 23, 1850, Burn sent calculations for rebuilding Sandon. He considered 'as there is a quarry in the near neighbourhood which promises to afford a sufficient supply of stone for the simple cost of working … I am of the opinion that a saving of from four to five thousand pounds might thereby be judiciously expected'. Burn's estimate of £28,500 could thus be reduced to 'not more than £24,000'. Less than delighted by this saving, Lady Harrowby wrote to her son, exclaiming 'all the fat is in the fire as I expected, we shall have to begin again *de novo*'.

By the end of 1850, to the relief of all concerned, a scheme had been decided upon and Burn's office was engaged in preparing duplicate sets of coloured working drawings. By January 1851 the task was complete, and the clients could now see the house that they were about to build. But doubts were again surfacing, and on January 18 Burn wrote to inform them that, following a request from Lord Harrowby, he had succeeded in increasing the projection of the drawing room to 18 feet. Having dutifully made this alteration, he subtly reminded his client that '(the revision) has compelled an alteration of every plan and of the end elevation and sections', but conceded, 'I think it is well worth the time I extended [sic] on them'.

On 2 April 1851 Burn wrote providing reassurance that his methods of securing the outer and inner faces of masonry would be sufficient, and advised that with the specification now written, he was ready to apply to tradesmen for estimates. His eagerness to proceed was not unreasonable, but it was premature, and it must have been a frustration to be required to prepare a further revised set of drawings. A pair of shaped gables to the garden front and a single storey projection within the southwest corner of the private wing were now to be altered or omitted. Three months later all drawings were complete, a suitable contract price secured, and builders from Ayr in Scotland were appointed. On Lord Sandon's 21st birthday, January 16, 1852, three and a half years after the fire, the foundation stone was finally laid and productive building commenced – which lasted eight days. Burn now found himself contemplating a further significant alteration.

It was common for Burn's houses to have symmetrically composed garden façades, typically with a recessed centre four to five bays wide.[8] This arrangement was proposed for Sandon, but with a centre of eight bays' width (coupled with

Fig. 5 | Elevation of the south façade. January 24, 1852

large expanses of plate glass) and he was aware the formula was pushed beyond its aesthetic boundaries. To counter this potentially bleak centre, on January 24, 1852 the elevation had been altered, and now had a slightly advanced central square bay with shaped gable over (Fig. 4). By May 6 this had been revised to a canted bay arrangement with shaped gable above, which echoed the flanking bays. Satisfied this proposal added the required gravitas, Burn completed working drawing No. 84 (Fig. 5) – clearly he and his office had been busy – and began the preparation of a perspective view. Then, following some communication from Lord Harrowby, the perspective drawing was inscribed 'unfinished'[Fig. 6]. On May 11 Burn wrote 'I understand there is now to be no alteration whatever on the south front (Bow Windows or otherwise) ... I conceived it was your ... particular wish and desire to have the long south front improved ... and this the centre bow most effectually accomplished ... I have no personal feeling or desire to have (the bow) executed ... and I proceed as directed'. His last statement is important, for it displays a surprising deference over significant architectural elements, and consequently an occasion where his desire to oblige adversely affected his design. He was wrong to have conceded, as the unbroken regiment of openings resulted in the south front being the least successful element of the house (Fig. 7).

In July Burn's principal assistant, William Colling, was answering correspondence from the Earl and Countess, arguing against Lord Sandon's suggestion that coloured shields be added to the south façade, as well as advising Lady Harrowby on the design of plasterwork. But suggestions by Lady Harrowby of 26 January, 1853, concerning the improvement of the domestic accommodation (at a time when the shell of the house was complete), demanded Burn's full attention, and were firmly rebuffed. 'I went over the whole matter of the proposed alterations ... with Lord Harrowby yesterday and believe I satisfied his Lordship that the changes of the Butler's pantry to a store room would be most injudicious, and result in permanent discomfort and inconvenience.' The proposed plate scullery was dismissed as 'utterly useless', and criticism that the designated area for wine storage was inadequate countered: 'if more binnage is required, there are vacant cellars enough to hold any quantity of wine that could be desired'. As for the 'flour room', Burn could 'see no case for it whatever, as a binn (sic) in the Bake house is all that is necessary, and as much as nine out of ten Private bakehouses ever have'.

By September 29, 1853 Burn had returned sketches prepared by Lady Harrowby. Now under consideration, at least as far as Lady Harrowby was concerned, was the addition of a coat of arms over the portico. Burn took the line that the arms 'would be ultimately destructive to the architectural effect and appearance of the portico, and that any breaking of the main cornice ... would be ruinous to the whole design, and therefore quite impossible for me to attempt the working out

Fig. 6 | Working drawing of the south façade alteration, May 6, 1852

Fig. 7 | Perspective of the south façade, May 10, 1852

Sandon Hall, No 84,
Alteration of South Front, in accordance with Drawing No 83.
Elevation
and
Plan
6 Stratton Street
6th May 1852

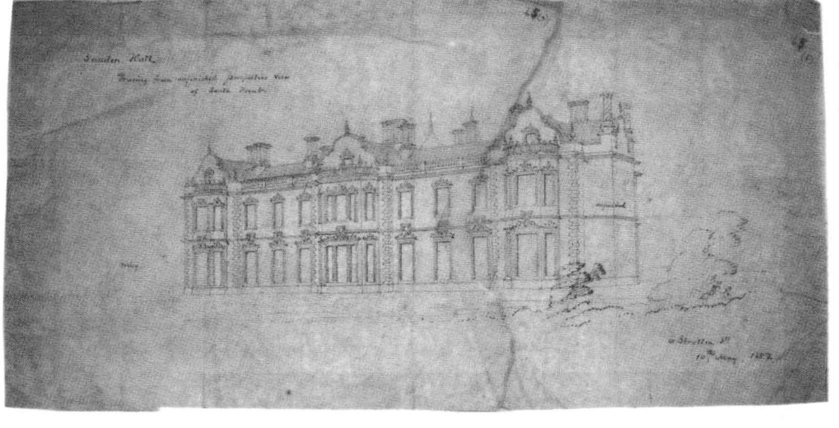

of'. Aware he had recently rejected a considerable number of 'improvements', he reiterated, in case it was not very apparent, 'I need not I hope say how anxiously I desire to study and unceasingly endeavour to realise every wish or suggestion ... and it is with the utmost pain and reluctance that on any point I express an opinion in opposition to them.' Consequently, the 'impossibility' of incorporating the arms had, by the end of the letter become possible, and dutifully he enclosed a sketch of 'what in my opinion should be done, and if that is not satisfactory I really know not what to do or recommend' (Fig.8).

On November 23, Burn was again deflecting alterations. The seemingly harmless addition of a water closet within the entrance hall was mooted. What caused Burn irritation was that this alteration had been suggested by Lord Sandon directly to Mr McLeish, the clerk of works, bypassing Burn altogether. Feeling he had 'no right to object to any arrangement or change of plan your Lordship may suggest', but 'impelled from a sense of duty, both to the comfort and construction of the building, and to my own character' he appealed to Lord Harrowby to reconsider. He was concerned that a water closet '2 feet wide, without space in front to turn or move ... would condemn (Burn) for ever as being ever fit for the arrangement of an ordinary cottage'. The aesthetics were also troubling, particularly the additional window for the water closet, which in overlooking the entrance Burn considered 'a sad deformity'.

Fig. 8 | Photograph of the south façade, 1860

The matter was temporarily dropped, and on December 20, 1853 designs for plasterwork were forwarded, which Burn prefaced by adding 'it is possible none of them may be precisely what you desire'. It was likely with the same pessimism that he sent sketches for the dining-room recess, panelling, chimney shafts and fireplaces, the majority of which remained unexecuted. The fact that one of the fireplace 'designs' was a brazen tracing from a book shows that, by this stage of the project, there was some creative detachment and unwillingness on Burn's part (Fig. 9). [9]

Only one letter survives from Burn written during 1854, and Colling again appears to have taken over at least some of the correspondence. But during June 1855 Burn received a letter from Lady Harrowby that he could not leave unanswered. The Countess had written, partly out of an understandable grievance that he had not replied to a letter sent by Lord Harrowby over one month ago, and partly to inform him that they had instructed the clerk of works to block up temporarily the windows within the entrance hall.[10] She could not have anticipated Burn's reaction: 'probably I may have erred in not replying to Lord Harrowby's letter ... but the truth is ... there are so many things done ... at Sandon, contrary to the advice I have given, and the drawings and suggestions I have submitted, I not only feel my presence there to be wholly useless, but as giving a sanction to arrangements and designs which my whole experience condemns

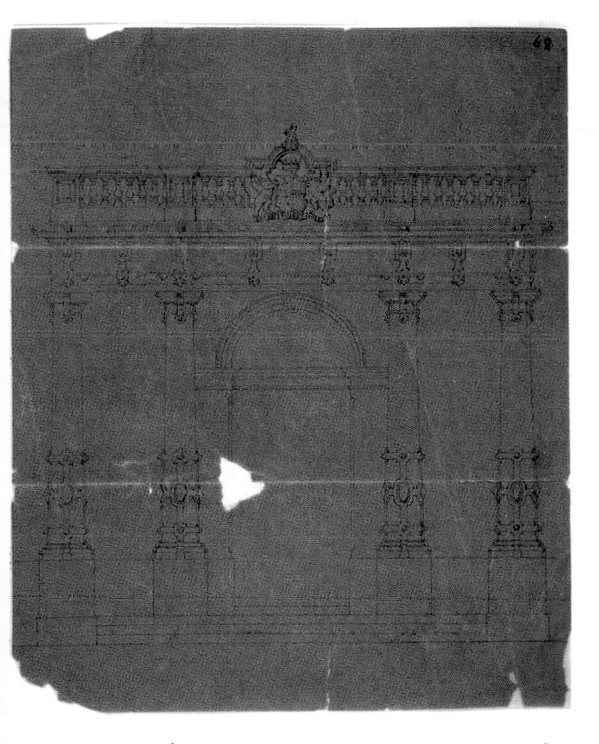

Fig. 9 | Undated drawing for the entrance porch

Fig. 10 | Tracing of a fireplace design, February 7, 1854

… and as these matters cannot but be distressing to me, and I can be no party to the shutting up of the windows of the Entrance Hall … I (have) no hesitation in coming to the determination of retiring from the Charge of the Works … there are things which I cannot do, even where my every inclination would prompt me only to oblige.'

Despite his resignation, which appears to have been refused (or perhaps Burn had been pacified), by August 23, 1855 he was giving instructions for the completion of the estate gasworks, and stating that he would provide advice about detailing to whoever was employed to execute the dining-room sideboard (Fig. 1).[11] But beneath the detached tone of Burn's letter, annoyance remained, and with it he readdressed the unresolved matter of the entrance windows. On learning these had been blocked as a permanent rather than temporary measure, he wrote requesting Lord Harrowby should reconsider the matter, stating: 'in my opinion … the whole character of the Entrance will be ruined without one window at least'. Fearing the battle already lost, Burn made a final attempt to have, at the very least, the west window reinstated, 'if that is universally condemned, I shall be perfectly willing to have the space plastered over at my own expense.' Feeling there was little more he could say or suggest, he validated his reasoning, 'your Lordship appears to think I attach unnecessary importance to this, and if I do it is for the character of the building, and what I believe to be essential to the comfortable occupation of the house'.

The same letter also criticised the timber fire surround in the entrance hall, which due to the complexities of the mouldings applied, Burn regretted would cost more than the good, plain marble one he had designed. Conflict regarding how the house should be finished moved to the oak floor of the entrance, which Lord Harrowby wished to be an intricate design – in opposing this Burn made his view clear: 'It has been my anxious study and desire, and the subject of constant labour to meet your Lordship's wishes, and on every occasion have given up my own opinion; in the arrangement of the elevations, the ceilings, and details in all quarters … I cannot visit Sandon with satisfaction if debarred from completing the entrance in the manner I have suggested'. In effect, Burn had tendered a second resignation, or at least an ultimatum: finish the entrance on my terms, or do without me. But Sandon was too near completion for this tactic to work, and the entrance hall was finished according to Lord Harrowby's wishes.

By August 1 Burn was asked to visit Sandon. He would offer no more than half a day of his time, and made it clear why he was attending 'It would be very desirable … that McLeish had all his accounts made up and prepared before I go to Sandon, as there forms the only material duty I have now to perform with reference to the works.' This, Burn's last letter in the archive, represents the final communication between him and his clients. In June 1855 the family's seven years of living at the inn in Sandon village came to an end, and they were able to spend their first night in the new house. With the project finally complete both parties must ultimately have felt they had made considerable sacrifices.

Burn did not universally ingratiate himself to clients, and his 'frank and plain spoken manner was not always tolerated.'[12] He was opinionated, but so too were his clients (which, to an extent, was their privilege) and consequently conflict was inevitable. To those who had not witnessed the battle of wills, Sandon appeared as a total success, and in reality what resulted was a dignified residence of definite character, with an interior well-proportioned and imaginatively detailed. However, Burn's clients remained less certain. In giving the first floor rooms names such as 'Spring' and 'Butterfly', Lord and Lady Harrowby succeeded, in a small way, in brightening the cloud that hung over the building process. Only one room was given a non-historical human dedication, and as a clear indication of the esteem in which they held their architect, they hung, over the door to the water closet, a nameplate inscribed 'W. Burn'.

NOTES

1. Between 1840 and 1850 Burn had built or substantially altered 40 country houses, in addition to commissions for 10 churches and a handful of civic buildings.
2. c.f. Falkland House, Fife (1839–44); Whitehill House, Midlothian (1839–44); Stoke Rochford Hall, Lincolnshire (1841–43); Rauceby Hall, Lincolnshire (1842); Revesby Abbey, Lincolnshire (1844–8); Dartrey, Co. Monaghan (1844–6); Calwich Abbey, Staffordshire (1846–50); Bangor Castle, Co. Down (1847); Idsworth House, Hampshire (1848–52); Poltalloch House, Argyllshire (1848–53); and Eastwell Park, Kent (1849, not completed by Burn).
3. The building of Calwich Abbey, an elegant Jacobethan country house designed by Burn in the same county as Sandon, may have further suggested his services.
4. Between 1845 and 1848 Cubitt designed Osborne House, Isle of Wight, for Queen Victoria, in an Italianate style.
5. Should this have remained the preference of his clients, Burn could have risen to the challenge, having five years earlier skilfully remodelled Prestwold Hall, Leicestershire, in such a fashion.
6. This drawing was superseded on 5 February 1852 by plan No 72, which comprehensively revised the layout of the forecourt wing accommodation.
7. Particularly the rebuilding of Buchanan Castle, Stirlingshire, destroyed by fire in 1850, for the Duke of Montrose.
8. For example, Falkland House and Poltalloch (four bay centres) and Stoke Rochford Hall (five bay centre).
9. Traced from the pages of Wendel Dietterlin's *Architectura,* a late-16th-century book of ornament.
10. A surprising alteration, given the Countess had desired a house with as much natural light as possible.
11. Given its bold baroque design, drawn from the pages of Dietterlin's *Architectura*, Burn's input was clearly considerable.
12. T.L. Donaldson, 'Memoir of the Late William Burn, Fellow', *Proceedings of the RIBA,* 1869–70, p. 124.

ACKNOWLEDGEMENTS

I am indebted to the Earl of Harrowby for allowing me, on numerous occasions, such unrestricted access to his home and archive. I owe a particular debt to Michael Bosson, Archivist and Manager at Sandon, for his help, his patience during my aimless wanderings about the house, and for his never-waning kindness over the years.

3 · Rail, steam and speed

GAVIN STAMP

Railways, steam ships and even air travel had their beginnings in the 1840s and faster travel brought new opportunities and challenges to architecture. In terms of communications, the modern world was created in the 1840s, and in Britain.

During the summer of 1851, some six million people visited the Great Exhibition in Hyde Park. This number – almost a third of the population of Great Britain - was a tribute to the scale and efficiency of the British railway system, as most visitors travelled to London by train. Ten years earlier, such mass transit would not have been possible. The first steam-hauled passenger railway had been the Liverpool and Manchester, opened in 1830, but it was during the 1840s, that the skeleton of the railway system still in use today was created – entirely by private enterprise. It was in this difficult and contradictory decade that the railway changed perceptions of distance, making far-flung parts of the United Kingdom much more accessible by achieving 'the annihilation of space by time'.[1] It was also during the 1840s that crossing the Atlantic by steamboat became a practicable possibility and – most surprisingly – that the notion of travel in a heavier-than-air flying machine first gripped the public imagination.

At the beginning of that decade, there was only one trunk railway line open to the north out of London: the London & Birmingham, engineered by Robert Stephenson. Connections with the Grand Junction Railway to Liverpool and Manchester and with the North Midland Railway from Derby to Leeds made it possible to travel by rail as far as Lancaster on the west side of the Pennines and to York on the east, but no further. In 1840, there were virtually no railways open in the West Country or East Anglia, or in Wales or Scotland (Edinburgh and Glasgow were finally joined by rail in 1842, and the calotypes of Linlithgow taken by Hill and Adamson three years later would seem to make the town's railway station on that line the first ever to be photographed; Fig. 3). Brunel's stupendous Great Western was running only as far as Swindon and the only main line south of the Thames was Joseph Locke's London and Southampton.

By the end of the decade, however, it was possible to travel from Plymouth to Aberdeen entirely by railway, and after 1846 A.W.N. Pugin could reach his new house at Ramsgate by train rather than by steamboat down the Thames. Although a few individuals, such as Colonel Sibthorpe, MP for Lincoln, continued to

Fig.1 | The interior of Newcastle Central Station by John Dobson, architect, 1846–50; detail of a photograph, *c.*1860 [National Railway Museum]

oppose railways – calling them 'public frauds and private robberies', which 'had materially increased the distress of the country' – they had in fact conquered the whole of society.[2] Notwithstanding some public anxiety, Queen Victoria made her first railway journey in 1842, returning from Windsor on the Great Western from Slough to Paddington. By the middle of 1850 there were 6,308 miles of railway in operation in the United Kingdom and some 2,436 steam locomotives working on them. During the preceding year, these railways had carried 66.8 million passengers – 7.7 million of them in first-class carriages – which was twice as many as had been carried in 1845. The receipts enjoyed by the railway companies in 1850 for passenger travel were £6.5 million, and for goods, cattle and mail some £5.9 million.[3]

The extent of the British railway system, and its topographical impact, by the year of the Great Exhibition may be gauged from Edward Churton's *Railroad Book of England*. This was published in 1851, by which date time itself had also conformed to railway practice, as – to facilitate the timetable – railway time had become standard time throughout Britain. This was possible owing to the electric telegraph, invented by Charles Wheatstone and William Fothergill Cooke in 1837, which was laid alongside the tracks. 'There was even railway time observed in clocks, as if the sun itself had given in', wrote Charles Dickens in 1846.

Fig. 2 | London Bridge Station in 1851: the South Eastern Railway's terminus on the left designed by Samuel Beazley, 1850–51, and the entrance to the London, Brighton & South Coast Railway's platforms on the right (both demolished); steel engraving from *Tallis's Illustrated London; in commemoration of The Great Exhibition ...*, London & New York, *c.* 1851

'Wonderful Members of Parliament, who, little more than twenty years before, had made themselves merry with the wild railroad theories of engineers, and given them the liveliest rubs in cross examination, went down into the north with their watches in their hands, and sent on messages before by the electric telegraph, to say that they were coming.'[4] George Bradshaw produced his first *Bradshaw's Railway Guide* in December 1841, although railway timetables had been published for some years before this. Excursion trains are almost as old as the railways themselves, but it is worth noting that Thomas Cook commenced his great touring enterprise by hiring a special train, from Leicester to Loughborough, and back, in 1841.

The Railway Mania, that orgy of over-heated speculation in 1845–47, may have led to economic recession and the ruination of, amongst many others, Gilbert Scott's erstwhile partner William Bonython Moffatt, but there was no stopping railway construction. For all his dubious methods, Edward Hudson, the 'Railway King', succeeded in his aim of making all the railways come to York in so far as he placed the city on the east coast route to Scotland. Rail travel from Euston to Edinburgh became possible in 1849 with the openings of Stephenson's High Level Bridge across the Tyne and the Royal Border Bridge, that noble viaduct across the Tweed. The Great Northern Railway from Doncaster down to Kings Cross was running throughout only just in time for the Great Exhibition. Travel to Scotland up the west coast by rail was achieved a little earlier, in 1847, rendering the contemporary development of Fleetwood in Lancashire by Decimus Burton somewhat superfluous. Presumably never imagining that the railway could ever conquer the steep climb over Shap to Carlisle, Sir Peter Hesketh-Fleetwood had created a port from which ferries left for Ardrossan to connect with the railway to Glasgow, allowing passengers from London to stay at the North Euston Hotel overnight.[5]

Faster travel to Ireland also became possible with the opening of the Chester and Holyhead Railway throughout in 1850, crossing the Menai Strait on the tubular iron spans of the Britannia Bridge [Fig. 4], by which, as Alexander 'Greek' Thomson put it, tendentiously, 'Stephenson laid a lintel over the opening formed by the sea between Caernarvon and the island of Anglesey which is considerably greater than any opening ever spanned by an arch.'[6] The controversial collapse of the cast-iron Dee Bridge at Chester under a train on this line in 1847, which killed five people and for which Stephenson nobly but unfairly took responsibility, was a reminder that progress and experiment came at a cost.

Although the first trunk lines were begun in the previous decade it was in the 1840s that the landscape of Britain was dramatically transformed by such heroic bridges, as well as by the viaducts, cuttings, tunnels and other earthworks necessary to achieve the gentle gradients that the slow-climbing early steam locomotives required. Such structures inspired both awe and admiration among the public, leading to the publication of prints and books illustrating and describing the railway lines that continued to be published right through the decade – the finest being the *History and Description of the Great Western Railway* with its lithographs by John C. Bourne published in 1846, a sequel to the same artist's *London and Birmingham Railway* of 1839.

By 1850, journeys were measured in hours rather than days. Edinburgh could be reached from London in 12 hours, Plymouth in seven hours. The fastest timetabled speeds – in the world, of course – were achieved on the Great Western. Turner's celebrated painting of 1845, *Rain, Steam and Speed*, depicts a Great Western train crossing Brunel's red-brick elliptical arched bridge at Maidenhead. This was owing both to the locomotives designed by Daniel Gooch, with their seven-foot single driving wheels, and the comfortable engineering of Brunel's broad-gauge main line. Working from first principles rather than adopting the conventional Northumbrian mining gauge of 4 feet 8½ inches inherited by the

Fig.3 | One of a series of the earliest surviving photographs of a railway station: Linlithgow, with the station on the Edinburgh & Glasgow Railway, opened 1842, in the foreground; calotype by D.O. Hill & R. Adamson, 1845. [Glasgow University]

Fig.4 | Robert Stephenson's Britannia Tubular Bridge, showing the floating of the second tube, 3rd December 1849 (bridge since mutilated); lithograph by George Hawkins, 1850 [Courtesy of the Ironbridge Gorge Museum Trust - Elton Collection: AE185.819]

Fig.5 | The Welwyn Viaduct on the Great Northern Railway, Joseph Cubitt, engineer, 1848–50; watercolour by W. Humber, 1850 [Courtesy of the Ironbridge Gorge Museum Trust - Elton Collection: AE185.164]

Stephensons, Brunel argued that a gauge of 7 feet between the rails would give a faster and smoother ride [Fig. 6]. In the 1840s, this was undoubtedly true.

In competitive tests undertaken for the Royal Commission established to examine the gauge question in 1845, Gooch's locomotives pulling six six-wheeled carriages maintained an average speed of 50 mph, while one of the Stephenson's North Midland Railway engines ran so badly it came off the track. Nevertheless, the following year Parliament was advised that the 'narrow' gauge should become the standard for Great Britain. Two gauges within a small island could not be sustained, and while it was possible to convert broad to narrow with ease, widening tunnels and bridges was prohibitively expensive. Besides, the inconvenience to passengers of having to change trains where the gauge changed, as notoriously they had to do at Gloucester, was easily demonstrated. Even so, Brunel's noble broad gauge lived on in the west of England until 1892.

The carriages these trains hauled were mostly short, with four wheels and typically consisting of three compartments; their external appearance proclaiming their descent from the stage coach. Such vehicles gave neither a quiet nor a smooth ride. Some were longer, wider and better running. 'Beyond all doubt,' considered Hamilton Ellis, 'the very best ordinary carriages in the early eighteen-forties were the four-compartment, six-wheeled first class of the Great Western Railway, running on 7 ft. gauge'.[7] The carriages the Great Western reluctantly provided for third-class passengers, however, were not so comfortable and were often little better than cattle trucks. In 1844 an act promoted by W. E. Gladstone,

GREAT WESTERN RAILWAY.
BY
J.C.BOURNE.

then President of the Board of Trade, obliged all the companies to run a daily 'Parliamentary' train for third-class passengers at a cost of penny a mile in carriages with seats in which they would be protected from the elements 'as far as consistent with the necessary admission of light and air', although open roofless carriages continued to be used on other trains for some years yet.[8]

These early carriages were far from safe, as they easily disintegrated in accidents, of which there were many. Charles Barry was injured in one in 1844.[9] Even though it was estimated in 1851 that the chance of being killed while travelling by rail was 1 in 420,437, the public was alarmed by the number of exploding locomotives, derailments and collisions – for signalling was then in its infancy.[10] Acts passed in 1840 and 1842 allowed the Board of Trade to recruit railway inspecting officers both to inspect and approve new lines and to investigate the causes of accidents, and these men, recruited from the Royal Engineers, slowly but steadily forced improved safety measures on the complacent and parsimonious railway companies.[11] A dreadful accident at Meudon on the line from Paris to Versailles in 1842, in which the train caught fire and claimed the lives of 57 people, including the explorer J.-S.-C. Dumont d'Urville, alerted Sydney Smith to the danger of the policy of the Great Western in locking carriage doors between stations. 'We have been, up to this point, very careless of our railway regulations', he wrote in a letter to the *Morning Chronicle*. 'The first person of rank who is killed will put everything in order, and produce a code of the most careful rules. I hope it will not be one of the bench of bishops; but should it be so destined, let the burnt bishop – the unwilling Latimer – remember that however painful gradual concoction by fire may be, his death will produce unspeakable benefit to the public. Even Sodor and Man will be better than nothing.'[12]

The rapid expansion of the railway system had two positive consequences for architecture. One was increased ease of movement, enabling London-based architects to acquire and supervise many more jobs. When the young Scott and Moffatt were energetically competing for Union workhouse commissions all over England after the 1834 Poor Law Amendment Act, they had to travel by stage-coach. Thirty years on, Scott wrote: 'one wonders, in these self-indulgent days, how we could stand the travelling all night outside coaches in the depth of winter, and in all weathers ... These were the last days of the integrity of the old coaching system ... It was a splendid perfection of machinery, but its fate was sealed, the great lines of railway being in rapid progress.'[13] It was in the 1840s that Scott was able to establish his legendary habit of rushing all over Britain by train from the Spring Gardens office in London, using the many hours spent in railway carriages to draft his reports or to write letters. Similarly Pugin, who once described himself as a 'locomotive being', could barely wait for a new railway

Fig.6 | The frontispiece of *The History and Description of the Great Western Railway* by John C. Bourne, 1846, showing one of Daniel Gooch's 7 ft single passenger locomotives emerging from the western portal of the Bristol No.1 tunnel (since removed), designed by I.K. Brunel.

to open before he could travel on it, off to inspect another new church under construction.[14]

The other, more obvious, consequence was the many commissions for station buildings and the other structures required by the railways. As the railways were always anxious to mollify an anxious and sometimes hostile public, attention was at first paid to making the new railways as attractive as possible and architects were employed almost from the beginning. The division between architects and engineers was less wide than it became later in the century and this first, heroic generation of railway engineers seems to have had an instinctive aesthetic sense when dealing with masonry structures. Nevertheless, even with the simplest viaducts required an architectural draughtsman to compose suitably Roman cornices and imposts. Many architects also acted as surveyors and undertook railway work and when a building was required for public use at a railway station, the employment of an architect became essential.

In the 1840s, a number of architects came to specialise in railway work. There was G.T. Andrews, who was closely associated with Hudson in the north-east; Sancton Wood, who worked for the Eastern Counties Railway amongst other companies; David Mocatta on the London & Brighton; and Francis Thompson, who worked for Robert Stephenson in the north-west. Above all, there was the prolific and intriguing William Tite, who was employed by Joseph Locke when he engineered the London & Southampton, the Lancaster & Carlisle and many other lines – including the line from Paris to Rouen and Le Havre; he was also architect to the Caledonian Railway in Scotland. Tite was responsible for many stations as well as making drawings for structures along the way. He acted as both surveyor and architect and did so well financially that he invested in railways and became a director of several companies. Some railway engineers, notably Brunel, had

Fig.7 | Bricklayers' Arms Station, Bermondsey, by Lewis Cubitt, 1843–44 (demolished); woodcut from *The Pictorial Times* for December 13, 1845 [Roger Cline]

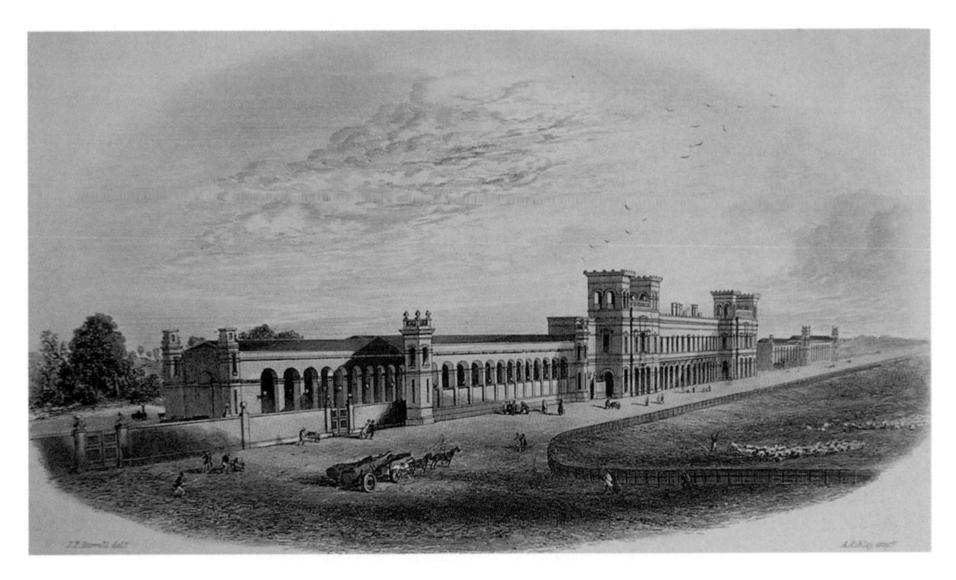

Fig.8 | Chester General Station by Francis Thompson; drawn by J.F. Burrell, engraved by A. Ashley, *c.* 1848. [Courtesy of the Ironbridge Gorge Museum Trust - Elton Collection: AE185.691]

architectural pretensions, but because of their sheer scale and complexity, the creation of a railway line had to be a collaborative effort. Even Brunel, tireless and domineering as he was, could not have had the time to design every structure on the lines engineered. Adrian Vaughan has shown that he employed several rather dim architects, such as William Westmacott, on Temple Meads, and John Gandell, to draw out and detail his railway buildings.[15]

The precise working relationship between architects and engineers on railway projects merits further investigation. The architect would have to be briefed by the engineer about the layout of railway tracks, platforms and the facilities required. If an iron train shed was to be constructed, this would usually be delegated to an assistant engineer, although Brunel was closely involved with the design of his overall timber roofs on the Great Western. At Chester, for instance, the station roof was strictly utilitarian and was designed by Charles Wild, not by Thompson, the architect of the station building. At Newcastle Central, however, Robert Stephenson had very little to do with the design of the station and the overall triple-span roof, of rolled wrought-iron arches [Fig. 1], as well as the magnificent long façade seems to have been the creation of that fine local architect John Dobson. Dobson also detailed the masonry piers supporting Stephenson's High Level Bridge across the Tyne, just as Francis Thompson designed the powerful stone piers for the Britannia and Conway bridges in north Wales. As John Rapley has written, 'The roll of famous architects employed on railway work does not include the sort of men who would be subservient to any engineer'.[16] On the other hand, it is important to remember, as Gordon Biddle points out, that 'in the early years there was no clear distinction between architects, engineers and surveyors; it was not until the mid nineteenth century that quite separate professions began to form'.[17]

When Euston was designed in the mid-1830s, the contrast between the great Doric propylaeum and the simple train sheds sited asymmetrically behind suggested that the form a railway terminus should take was far from clear. By the 1840s, however, the characteristic form of both large urban and small village stations was rapidly evolving. Passengers needed shelter on the platforms, and a masonry building was required for a ticket office, waiting rooms and to give the station an architectural presence. That presence was usually Classical. Some of the larger stations resembled a Palladian mansion, complete with a portico. Huddersfield, by J.P. Pritchett both senior and junior (1847), sports a grand hexastyle Corinthian portico and for Gordon Biddle is 'the finest classical station in Britain.'[18] A more modest but more subtle example is at Monkwearmouth by

Fig.9 | Carlisle Station by William Tite; elevation in pen & watercolour, c.1847 [National Railway Museum]

Thomas Moore (1848), where the tetrastyle portico is Greek Ionic; 'If one does not mind a railway station looking like a Literary and Scientific Institution or a provincial Athenaeum', wrote Pevsner, 'then [it] is one of the most handsome early stations in existence.'[19]

Some of the more accomplished railway architects moved away from obvious prototypes, however, and produced distinctive railway buildings. The long, grand Classical front at Newcastle, John Dobson's masterpiece, could not possibly be mistaken for a country house or a town hall. At Chester, Francis Thompson designed the long frontage in an Italianate manner, in brick and stone, terminated by pavilions with twin belvederes on the roof [Fig. 5]; the inspiration was possibly Schinkel and Persius at Potsdam. Chester's frontage was wide because the station originally had one long through platform for trains in both directions. This arrangement still survives today at Cambridge, where the station building is an Italianate arcade – all fifteen of whose arches were originally open. This design has been attributed to both Francis Thompson and to Sancton Wood.[20]

The latter was also responsible for the magnificent palazzo which is Kingsbridge, or Heuston Station, in Dublin – a city which, with J. S. Mulvany's Broadstone Station, can now boast more and grander railway architecture of the 1840s than any city in Great Britain.

Not all these stations were Classical. Brunel's Great Western terminus at Temple Meads was designed in Tudor Gothic in deference to the perceived antiquity of Bristol; Tite's station for Hampton Court is Jacobean in style and he designed in Tudor in places on the London and South Western's system, the station at Windsor with its royal waiting room is the best, while his important station buildings at Carlisle and Perth were Tudor Gothic. The Midland Railway's Stamford Town, by Sancton Wood, is a particularly charming Gothic design, but perhaps the most elaborate Gothic buildings of the decade were on the London and Croydon Railway. Designed by the antiquarian architect Raphael Brandon (in association with the company's architect W.H. Brakespear) and built in 1845, these were not conventional stations but new engine-houses on a pre-existing line required in connection with the extraordinary experiment of atmospheric traction.[21]

The atmospheric railway, which enjoyed a brief but expensive vogue in the 1840s, was intended to do away with noisy, smelly and dangerous steam locomotives and provide silent, fast travel, a dream that could only be realised effectively with the advent of the electric motor. Instead of being pulled by a mobile steam engine, the leading car of the train was attached to a piston in a 15-inch diameter iron tube placed between the conventional rails, and this was propelled by an atmospheric vacuum created by stationary pumping engines

Fig.10 | Norwood station and engine-house on the London & Croydon atmospheric railway designed by Raphael Brandon with W.H. Brakespeare, 1845 (demolished); woodcut from *ThePictorial Times* for August 2, 1845 [Roger Cline]

placed at regular intervals along the line. The engine-houses, each containing a stationary steam-engine, were designed in the manner of a medieval barn while the necessary chimneys resembled a tall Gothic spire or minaret [Fig. 10]. For a time, the system, developed by Clegg & Samuda, worked between West Croydon and Forest Hill, then called Dartmouth Arms, and speeds of up to 75 mph were recorded. However, a regular service could not be sustained, and the system was abandoned in 1847.

In retrospect, the problems of keeping the tube airtight, let alone the difficulties of stopping the train in the right place and the nightmare complications of points and junctions, make it seem remarkable that the system was ever tried at all, but in the optimistic and experimental 1840s several distinguished engineers were briefly carried away by enthusiasm for its merits. One was Brunel, who recommended it for the South Devon Railway in 1844 as 'stationary power, if free from the weight and friction of any medium of communication, as a rope, must be cheaper, is more under command, and is susceptible of producing much higher speeds than Locomotive power.'[22] To provide the power, engine houses were built with Italianate details taken from Tuscan churches and the chimneys were campaniles. The system ran eventually between Exeter and Newton Abbot for about a year until it was replaced by locomotive power in 1848, the chief problem being the rapid decay of the greased leather flap over the piston slot which kept the tube airtight. It was, perhaps, the most embarrassing failure in Brunel's career, and one which cost railway investors dear.

The South Devon Railway was an extension of the Bristol and Exeter Railway, which was itself an extension of the original Great Western main line, and it enabled broad-gauge trains to reach Plymouth by 1849. But although Devon and Cornwall had been the objectives of the Great Western, Brunel always had another more distant destination in mind, having remarked to the directors back in 1835 when one of them commented on the immense length of the line, 'Why not make it longer, and have a steamboat to go from Bristol to New York, and call it the *Great Western*?'[23] Paddle steamers had been operating on rivers and around Britain's coasts since 1809 when Henry Bell launched his *Comet* on the Clyde, but it was assumed that no steamship could carry enough coal to cross the Atlantic. Brunel was one of those who realised that while the surface of a ship's hull offering resistance to the water was the square of its dimensions, its capacity for carrying coal and cargo was its cube. Greater efficiency could therefore be achieved by building a larger ship. Launched in 1837, Brunel's S.S. *Great Western*, launched in 1837 and, at 212 feet long, the largest ship in the world, nearly became the first steamship to cross the Atlantic – from Bristol to New York – the following year, taking 15 days, but it was beaten by a matter of hours by the smaller *Sirius*, an Irish ferry operated by the British & American Steam Navigation Co.

Following this success, the Great Western Steam-Ship Company commissioned another ship from Brunel. This was to be SS *Great Britain*. It was even larger and had an iron hull laid down, in Bristol, in 1839. While it was under construction, Brunel became aware that ships could be driven by the screw propeller, invented by Francis Pettit Smith. The paddle-wheels were scrapped and the vessel that was launched in 1844 was not only the largest ship in the world, over 300 feet long with a beam of 50 feet, but driven by a screw propeller designed by Brunel. The following year the *Great Britain* made her maiden voyage, crossing from Liverpool to New York in the record time of 14 days and 21 hours. This splendid vessel – today restored and preserved in Bristol – subsequently ran into difficulties, but the superiority of screw propulsion was demonstrated: with its iron hull and watertight bulkheads, it was the first modern ship. Even the deeply conservative Admiralty took notice, and in 1845, in an absurd test, HMS *Rattler*, equipped with a screw, hauled a naval paddle-steamer backwards at 2.8 knots. Brunel, as Adrian Vaughan wrote, 'was the first man in the world to develop the crude principle of the Archimedean screw propeller into a science, and mate it with iron hull and large engines. He was instrumental in introducing the propeller to the Royal Navy and is the founding genius of the ocean liner. This must be his greatest contribution to humanity.'[24]

Despite these two innovative Bristol-built ships, the Great Western Steamship Company was not a viable concern and was superseded by the British and North American Royal Mail Steam Packet Company, founded by a Canadian, Samuel Cunard. For most of the decade, Cunard enjoyed a monopoly of the transatlantic steamer trade until he was challenged by the advent of the United States Mail Steamship Company, or Collins line, in 1850. Cunard's ships were not as innovative as the Great Western's Bristol-built vessels, but they maintained a good safety record at a time when loss of life to fires and other disasters at sea was frequent. Cunard operated wooden-hulled paddle steamers, built on the Clyde. In 1850, the *Asia,* which could carry 150 first-class passengers, 30 second, a crew of 112 and 890 tons of coal all within her 267 foot length and 40 foot beam, crossed from Liverpool to Halifax in under nine days and, later that same year, from New York to Liverpool in just over 10 days at an average speed of 12.36 knots.[25] A visit to America was now not such a daunting prospect as it had been for the many unfortunates who emigrated from Britain and Ireland during the preceding decade crammed into sailing vessels.

In the course of the 1840s, steam-power changed the perception of time and space. The railway system conquered natural obstacles such as rivers and hills to unify the kingdom and, at the same time, the oceans began to be traversed by passenger-carrying steam-boats. It now even seemed possible to conquer the air. Man had first risen from the ground in a hot-air balloon in 1783 in Paris and by the 1840s coal-gas filled balloons in the sky were a reasonably familiar sight, although their descent in the countryside could still create consternation. Most of these ascents, however, were in the manner of stunts: controlled-direction air travel was not yet possible. The leading British showmen aeronauts were George Graham and his intrepid wife, Margaret (who survived numerous and regular accidents), and Charles Green.[26] The latter's most celebrated flights were made in an extra-large balloon, with a capacity of 70,000 cubic feet, called *The Vauxhall Royal Balloon*, which first ascended from the eponymous London pleasure ground in 1836. Later that year, Green's balloon ascended from London eventually to land in Germany, in the Duchy of Nassau; it was then renamed the *Royal Nassau*. The impact of this epic journey on the public is suggested by the fact that the 'Flight of the Monster Balloon' was still being exhibited in 14 pictures in Gordon's British Diorama on the Mound in Edinburgh in 1842. Two years later, Green estimated that he had made 299 ascents, 13 of them at night, and had carried 548 passengers, 28 of them women. By 1852, when he made his final ascent from Vauxhall, he had made over 500 flights.[27]

Such flights, however, were subject to the vagaries of the weather and, because of the prevailing wind, most ascents from London ended in the fields of Essex, where farmers became so exasperated with the damage caused to their property that they issued a proclamation in 1853 threatening aeronauts with dire penalties for trespass. Despite several attempts in Britain, a dirigible balloon – one that was powered and could be steered – had to wait until the Frenchman Henri Giffard took off from the Paris Hippodrome in his steam-powered, propeller-driven airship in 1852. The possibilities of flight in general had, however, already caught the imagination of the British public so that in the 1840s an optimistic proposal for a heavier-than-air passenger-carrying flying machine seemed, for a time, to be a practicable possibility.

In 1843, the Aerial Transit Company was launched in London and sought investors for the development of a proposal by W. S. Henson, assisted by John Stringfellow, for a steam-powered monoplane patented the previous year. This had been inspired by the aeronautical researches and experiments of Sir George Cayley. 'An Invention has recently been discovered,' began the prospectus, 'which if ultimately successful will be without parallel even in the age which introduced to the world the wonderful effects of gas and steam.'[28] For a few months, Henson's Aerial Steam Carriage generated a flurry of publicity – and ridicule; lithographs showing the *Ariel* flying over London [Fig. 12], over the pyramids of Egypt and elsewhere appeared, and similar prints were published in France and Germany. The company, however, failed to secure its Act of Incorporation and, discouraged, Henson eventually emigrated to the United States.

Nevertheless, C. H. Gibbs-Smith, the historian of aviation, considered that the Aerial Steam Carriage design was 'in most essentials ... the modern aeroplane, brain-born more than half a century before it could be realised in reality'.[29] Perhaps what is most significant is that, such was the technological optimism

Fig.11 | The earliest surviving photograph of a ship: I.K. Brunel's SS *Great Britain* in Bristol following her launch in 1843; calotype by Henry Fox Talbot, April/May 1844 [National Maritime Museum]

Fig.12 | William Henson's proposed Aerial Steam Carriage, the *Ariel*, flying over London; lithograph for the Aerial Transit Company by W.L. Walton, 1843 [Science Museum]

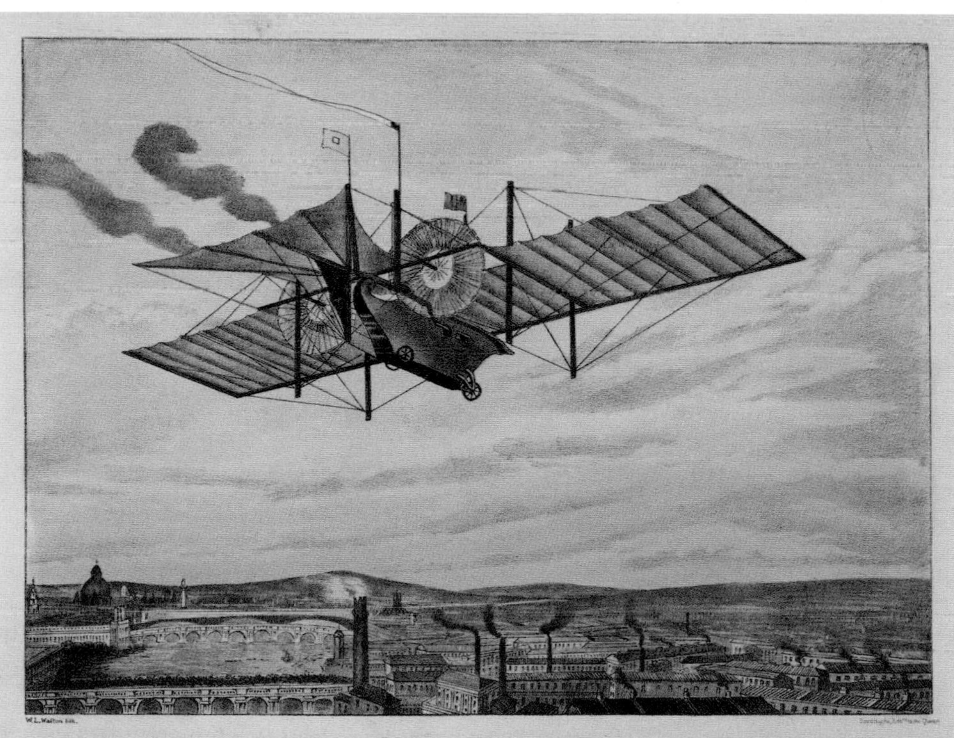
W. L. Walton lith.
By permission of the Patentees
THIS ENGRAVING of the FIRST CARRIAGE, the "ARIEL",
is respectfully inscribed, to the Directors of
THE AERIAL TRANSIT COMPANY,
by their obedient Servants
The Publishers.
London, Pub. March 28th 1843 by Ackermann & Co. Strand.

of the decade, many people took this project seriously. An article in *The Times* concluded that it was 'high time to begin to consider in a spirit of cheerful hope what will be the changes, commercial, social, and political, which the possession of this new-born power will necessarily bring about'.[30] Furthermore, Stringfellow continued with his experiments and, in 1848, the year of revolutions, his 12-foot span model monoplane, driven by two propellers powered by a lightweight steam engine, successfully flew, first in a disused lace factory in Chard, Somerset, and subsequently in a covered space in the Cremorne Gardens in London. This was the first power-driven, self-supported flight in the history of the world, and it took place in Britain in the 1840s.

The decade was, in many ways, one of conflict and uncertainty, but it was clear to almost everyone that technical progress and faster transport were going to make the world a better place. In *Dombey and Son*, which appeared in 1846 at the height of the Railway Mania, Dickens describes the chaos and devastation caused by the building of a railway in London, an account based on the construction of the London and Birmingham line through Camden Town, before raising his hat only half ironically to the 'yet unfinished and unopened Railroad ... [which] ... from the very core of all this dire disorder, trailed smoothly away, upon its mighty course of civilisation and improvement'.[31] Sydney Smith's feelings were less mixed. Writing in 1842 he concluded that 'Railroad travelling is a delightful improvement of human life ... Everything is near, everything is immediate – time, distance, and delay are abolished.'[32]

NOTES

1. For the significance of this phrase and for much else, see Michael Freeman, *Railways and the Victorian Imagination*, New Haven and London, 1999, a brilliant book which is particularly illuminating about the 1840s.
2. Quoted in John W. Dodds, *The Age of Paradox. A Biography of England 1841–1851*, London, 1953, p. 216.
3. These figures are taken from W. Gaspey, *Tallis's Illustrated London*, London and New York, 1851, pp. 183 and 188.
4. Charles Dickens, *Dombey and Son*, London, 1848, p.155.
5. It was while staying in the North Euston Hotel at Fleetwood, designed by Decimus Burton, that Pugin wrote to Lord Shrewsbury that 'The abomination of desolation, a modern Greek Town is unsupportable. I am sitting in a Grecian coffee room, in the Grecian hotel with a Grecian mahogany table [&c., &c. ... .] Not a pointed arch within sight and everything new and beastly' – quoted in Philip Miller, *Decimus Burton 1800–1881*, London, 1981, p. 32.
6. Alexander Thomson, 'Art and Architecture' (The Haldane Lectures, 1874), quoted in Gavin Stamp (ed.), *The Light of Truth and Beauty: The Lectures of Alexander 'Greek' Thomson, Architect 1817–1875*, Glasgow, 1999, p. 169.
7. Hamilton Ellis, *Railway Carriages in the British Isles from 1830 to 1914*, London, 1965, p. 27.
8. Quoted ibid. p.35.
9. In writing to Pugin to ask his help at the Palace of Westminster in 1844, Barry referred to his bad leg, which had been injured in a railway accident: *ex inf.* Rosemary Hill.
10. F.S. Williams, *Our Iron Roads: their History, Construction and Social Influences*, London, 1852, pp.320–21, quoted in Freeman, op. cit. [note 1 above], p. 86.
11. See L.T.C. Rolt, *Red for Danger*, 2nd ed., London, 1966, p. 18ff.
12. Quoted in Hesketh Pearson, *The Smith of Smiths*, London, n.d., p. 292.

13. Gavin Stamp (ed.), *Personal and Professional Recollections by Sir George Gilbert Scott* [1879], Stamford, 1995, p. 84.

14. Letter to David Charles Read, postmarked 14 January 1841, British Architectural Library PUG/12/1. Pugin's diaries first record him travelling by rail, from York to Manchester and Liverpool, on 12 March 1836: see the transcript of the diaries in Alexandra Wedgwood, *A.W.N. Pugin and the Pugin Family*, London, 1985, p. 35.

15. Adrian Vaughan, *Isambard Kingdom Brunel: Engineering Knight-Errant*, London, 1991, p.126, quoting a letter from Brunel to Westmacott and concluding that 'The existing front of the 'Old Station' at Temple Meads and the fireplaces within are a joint production of Brunel and Westmacott.' Such discoveries were evidently made subsequent to the same author's *A Pictorial Record of Great Western Architecture,* Oxford, 1977.

16. John Rapley, 'Fresh Perceptions of a Great Engineer', in Adrian Jarvis and Kenneth Smith (eds), *Perceptions of Great Engineers II*, Liverpool, 1998, p. 98; also see John Addyman and Bill Fawcett, *The High Level Bridge and Newcastle Central Station*, Newcastle, 1999.

17. Gordon Biddle, 'Railway Architecture, Architects and Engineers', in R.W. Ambler (ed.), *The History and Practice of Britain's Railways: A New Research Agenda*, Aldershot and Brookfield, Vermont, 1999, p. 72.

18. Gordon Biddle, *Britain's Historic Railway Buildings*, Oxford, 2003, p. 441.

19. Nikolaus Pevsner, *The Buildings of England: County Durham*, Harmondsworth, 1953, p. 187.

20. Biddle, op. cit. [note 18 above], p. 191.

21. Charles Hadfield, *Atmospheric Railways: A Victorian Venture in Silent Speed*, Newton Abbot, 1967, p.121ff.

22. Quoted ibid, p. 144.

23. Isambard Brunel, *The Life of Isambard Kingdom Brunel, Civil Engineer*, London, 1870, p. 233.

24. Adrian Vaughan, *Brunel: An Engineering Biography*, Hersham, 2006, p. 118.

25. C. Mackenzie-Kennedy, *The Atlantic Blue Riband: Evolution of the Express Liner*, York, 1993, pp. 15–16.

26. Ascents by George Graham were rare after 1838, but, as L.T.C. Rolt records in *The Aeronauts: A History of Ballooning 1783–1903*, London, 1966, p. 113, 'his amazing wife continued her headlong career, bearing George a long succession of progeny in the intervals and styling herself 'Her Majesty's Aeronautè' or 'The Only English Female Aeronaut.' [...] The really amazing thing is that Margaret Graham should have soldiered on in this way for no less than thirty years without, it would seem, becoming any more skilled in the art of balloon management, and yet survived to die in her bed.' Pugin's diary for 23 August 1836 records that 'Mr. Graham fell from Baloon [*sic*]', some architectural historians making the blinkered assumption that this must refer to the elderly architect James Gillespie Graham: Wedgwood, op. cit. [note 14 above], pp. 35 and 77.

27. Rolt, ibid., p.131.

28. M.J.B. Davy, *Henson and Stringfellow: Their Work in Aeronautics*, London, 1931, p. 39.

29. C.H. Gibbs-Smith, *A History of Flying*, London, 1953, p. 114.

30. Quoted in Davy, op. cit. [note 28 above], p. 42; also see Harald Penrose, *An Ancient Air: A Biography of John Stringfellow of Chard, The Victorian Aeronautical Pioneer*, Washington, DC, 1989.

31. Dickens, op. cit. [note 4 above], p. 46.

32. Quoted in Pearson, op. cit. [note 12 above], p. 292.

ACKNOWLEDGMENTS

I should like to thank Michael Bailey, Julia Elton and Roger Cline for their help with finding the illustrations for this article.

4 · 'Our Own': Thomas Hope, A.J. B. Beresford Hope & the creation of the High Victorian style

MICHAEL HALL

In 1846 A.J. B. Beresford Hope, chairman of the Ecclesiological Society, took a decisive lead in the creation of what is now known as High Victorian Gothic. His conception of a modern, synthetic style was derived in large part from his father, Thomas Hope.

A perennial problem afflicting the study of British architecture is the way that a chronological division, the beginning of the Victorian period in 1837, has for so long been a barrier that has divided scholars. Very few architectural historians cross this boundary, and even fewer cross it with it ease. Virtually all the standard reference works on which they rely either end or (more rarely) begin around 1840, most notably John Summerson's volume in the Pelican History of Art, *Architecture in Britain 1530–1830* and Howard Colvin's *Biographical Dictionary of British Architects 1600–1840*. Rupert Gunnis's *Dictionary of British Sculptors* creeps forward to 1851, but other fundamental tools, such as *The Dictionary of English Furniture Makers* or Ian Bristow's *Architectural Colour in British Interiors* stop in 1840.[1] There are of course many sound practical reasons for this. The dramatic growth of building in the 19th century, the establishment of the architectural profession, and, in particular, the founding of the architectural periodical press (*The Builder* began publication in 1843) make the study of Victorian architecture in many ways a different discipline from the architectural history of previous periods. Scholarship on architecture before 1840 is necessarily based more exclusively on manuscript sources and is focused on attribution to a degree that is unnecessary for later buildings.

Less justifiably, there is still a sense lingering on from the time that architectural history was established as an academic discipline in the early 20th century that the division is also a barrier of taste: Victorian architecture was for most scholars in the first half of the 20th century, and beyond, a subject of lesser quality and interest than that of earlier periods. For example, writing in his *Dictionary*, Colvin declares that Charles Barry 'cannot be absolved from contributing to the coarsening of architectural taste that is apparent in the 1840s'.[2] Such attitudes explain, for example, the very different histories of the Georgian Group and Victorian Society, and indeed the very fact that the conservation of architecture before 1914 is addressed by two bodies that take 1837 as their point of separation.

Fig.1 | Alexander James Beresford Beresford Hope in a photograph by Ernest Edwards, *c.* 1864. © National Portrait Gallery, London

This issue is particularly significant for a study of the 1840s, since it is impossible to understand the achievements of that decade without a knowledge of the architectural debates in progress at the time that Victoria came to the throne. In terms of one of the most significant and long-lasting changes in British architecture in the 1840s, the rise of the Gothic revival, those antecedents have to be sought much further back. There are good reasons inherent in the very subject itself why historians have taken the 1830s as a natural point of departure for study of the Gothic revival. Much of the intellectual and emotional energy that was poured into it derives from the Oxford Movement, usually dated from John Keble's Assize Sermon at Oxford on 14 July 1833. It is an essential part of the self-created historiography of that movement that the Tractarians were reacting against a century and a half of spiritual lethargy in the Church of England. This has been challenged surprisingly recently by historians, most notably Peter Nockles, who has explored the continuities between the Tractarians and the High Church of the 18th century.[3] This has helped to prepare the ground for architectural historians to examine the way that many apparently distinctive aspects of the Victorian Gothic revival, from the attack on pew rents – and therefore pews themselves – to the renewed emphasis on frequency of communion, and therefore the greater importance of the chancel, need to be sought in the late 18th and early 19th centuries.[4] Even such a familiar part of the story of Victorian Gothic as the controversy about church restoration has its origins in the 18th century; few arguments over restoration in the 19th century were as bitter as the disputes provoked by James Wyatt's interventions in medieval cathedrals from the 1780s onwards.

Parallel with the views on Anglican history fostered by the Oxford Movement were the attitudes to Gothic architecture promoted by the ecclesiologists and, above all, by A.W.N. Pugin. Whereas the ecclesiologists could at least see merit in the High Church reforms in the 17th century that had encouraged a more sympathetic understanding of the country's medieval ecclesiastical inheritance, Pugin, working from a Roman Catholic viewpoint, regarded the entire history of the English church since the Reformation as one of decline and corruption. The approach to history with which he is usually associated, most influentially propagated in the two editions of *Contrasts*, in 1836 and 1841, was predicated on the idea of discontinuity, on the complete contrast of the past and the present.[5] Despite the fierce reaction against virtually all aspects of Victorian art and culture in the mid 20th century, historians of the Gothic revival, beginning with Kenneth Clark in 1928, have remarkably uncritically accepted Pugin's standpoint in *Contrasts*.[6] Until very recently it was customary to regard the Victorian Gothic revival as a return to medieval architectural forms that had nothing to do with Gothic of the intervening period. The evident continuities in High Church thought and practice that had found expression in Gothic design for three centuries before the Tractarians were ignored.[7]

More narrowly, the direction taken by the Gothic revival in the 1840s cannot be understood without placing it in the context of the vigorous debates about architectural style in the immediately pre-Victorian period. Here the historian encounters a second discontinuity, but this time immediately after the 1840s. The Great Exhibition of 1851 is usually taken to mark an important break, between the early Victorians and the mid Victorians, or, to use art-historical terminology, between early Victorian and High Victorian design. Although the term 'High Victorian' has been challenged – what, it has been asked, is 'Low Victorian'? – the way that it has been used since the 1960s to characterise a stylistic movement is too useful, and by now too deeply entrenched, to be abandoned. High Victorian Gothic is for us now, perhaps, the Victorian style *par excellence*: powerful, polychromatic and sometimes harsh in its bravura manipulation of forms, it resulted in buildings that more than any led to the words 'Victorian' and 'ugly' being interchangeable for so much of the 20th century. Yet, as I shall argue, the sources for that style have to be sought further back even than the 1840s: elements of both its ideology and practice can be traced to the designs and writings of Thomas Hope, the great Regency collector, patron and designer. It is ironic that Hope's own designs were rediscovered and popularised in the early 20th century by the same leaders of taste who turned so strongly against the Victorians.[8]

The morphology of the High Victorian style was defined by Paul Thompson in his monograph on William Butterfield (1971) and by Stefan Muthesius in *The High Victorian Style* (1972).[9] It was a deliberate attempt to create a new style, based on synthesising foreign and English Gothic sources, and on exploiting the potential of materials that were either new or more easily available, from brick, tile and terracotta to marble and granite. It was also, like the Pre-Raphaelite movement, with which it was in many ways a self-conscious parallel, a movement that sought to reform contemporary art and design by looking back to earlier and purer styles of art than those preferred by the preceding generation.[10] The ecclesiological and Puginian emphasis on the paradigmatic importance of 'Middle-Pointed' architecture gave way to a new appreciation of early Gothic design, moving the point of reference back from around 1300 to around 1200. Just at the moment when Puginian Gothic achieved its greatest triumph, in the Mediaeval Court at the Great Exhibition, work was beginning on the building that more than any other would undermine its hegemony, William Butterfield's All Saints, Margaret Street.

This advance of the Gothic revival, beyond what was felt to be the undue emphasis on archaeological models that had characterised Gothic design in the 1840s, was termed 'development'. This word, of great significance in intellectual life in the 1840s, links architectural changes with both religious and scientific thought. It originated in the Oxford Society for Promoting the Study of Gothic Architecture (OSPGA; from 1848 the Oxford Architectural Society), a university society founded in 1839.[11] It was here, in the 1840s, that three strands of mid-19th-century thought – architectural, religious and scientific – came together in the search for a new style. The concept of 'development' that was debated there was in origin theological, and was rooted in Roman Catholic thought. This tackled the problem of how to justify the promulgation of doctrines that were not part of the teachings of the early Church. The answer was that although revelation was complete at the time of the founding of the Church, understanding of it changed and developed through time under the guidance of the Church. The doctrine was expounded by J.H. Newman in his *Essay on the Development of Christian Doctrine*, published in 1845, two months after his reception into the Roman Catholic Church. For Newman, the doctrine had pointed the way out of Anglicanism, as it had made clear to him that the basis of the Church's authority could not lie at some point in the past, but only in the fully developed modern Church, which, it became clear to him, must be the Church of Rome.[12]

Newman, although never a member of the OSPGA, took a close interest in it. David Brownlee has persuasively argued that his ideas on development had an influence on debate within the society, although not in the way that Newman himself might have predicted.[13] The notion of development could well have been taken as a problem for the Gothic revival in its Anglican, ecclesiological form, which was based on the idea that the Church of England derived its authority from its apostolic descent from the primitive church, untouched by the Reformation. Gothic was the outward symbol of that continuity with the past. Yet for Newman, as he wrote in 1848, '[Gothic] was once the perfect expression of the Church's ritual in those places in which it was in use; it is not the perfect expression now.'[14] A solution to this problem was put forward by one of Newman's friends, the Oxford historian Edward Freeman, who in a lecture delivered in to the OSPGA (of which he was secretary) argued that architecture too developed through time, and was always the embodiment of the culture from which it sprang.[15] This clearly suggested that revivalism as understood by the ecclesiologists was misconceived; architecture must develop through time.

Newman was content simply to abandon Gothic as the Roman Catholic Church had abandoned it in the 16th century, and in his own architectural patronage he preferred Renaissance and Baroque styles as most suitable for post-Tridentine church plans and liturgy, or, as in the University Church, Dublin, an early Christian style that was easily adaptable to modern use, as Gothic appeared to him not to be. Yet Freeman used the notion of development to suggest that a modern style need not be Classical or Baroque – anathema to ecclesiological thought – but might instead be a developed form of Gothic. Freeman was evidently attracted to an idea that seemed to chime with his own Liberal ideals of progress, not something likely to appeal to Newman.

'Development' was also a potent word in the debates on ideas about evolution in the natural world. The book that took the concept from scientific thought to a topic of debate in educated drawing rooms was one of the most influential publications of the 1840s, Robert Chamberlain's best-selling *Vestiges of the Natural History of Creation*, published anonymously in 1844.[16] This popularised the notion of evolutionary change over long periods of time in the history of the universe and, most importantly, the development of species, which were no longer to be thought of as individual acts of creation by God. As Chambers put it, 'the inorganic has one final comprehensive law, Gravitation. The organic, the other great department of mundane things, rests in like manner on one law, and that is Development.'[17] It might be assumed that Tractarian thought would be hostile to such ideas but that was not the case. In his inaugural lecture as Lee's Reader in Medicine at Oxford in October 1845, 'The Bodily Nature of Man', Henry Acland used the evolutionary ideas articulated in *Vestiges* to argue that there was nothing irreligious in studying man as part of animal creation.[18] This impressed High Church opinion in Oxford. Newman's close friend Charles Marriott attended Acland's entire course of lectures, and the High Church weekly *The Guardian*, founded by Oxford Tractarians, declared its acceptance of ideas of evolutionary development in science. In 1854 Acland went on to commission one of the key buildings of developed Gothic, the Oxford Museum. Designed by Benjamin Woodward, with the encouragement of John Ruskin, the museum proclaims in its ornament a reconciliation of religion and science: visitors enter through a portal carved with an image of Adam and Eve.[19] The museum's didactic use of marbles and granites and of ornamental forms derived from nature was closely paralleled in churches. For the moment, scientific discoveries about the evolution of the rocks and of nature appeared to be supporting a religious understanding of God at work in creation.

Acland had a strong interest in architecture, and was one of the earliest members of the OSPGA. Oxford's important role in the way that religious and scientific ideas about 'development' were translated into a new architectural style was reinforced by the part that leading Gothic architects played in the society. The most significant was A.W.N. Pugin, who was a close friend of J.H. Bloxam, a fellow of Magdalen and a member of the society's committee (and also a good friend of Newman). In 1840, only a year after the society had been founded, Pugin met its members in Oxford and offered them casts of Gothic sculpture and other items from his collection.[20]

Ironically, given Newman's hostility to Pugin as an embodiment of all that he regarded as misconceived in the Gothic revival, it was Pugin who first put the new ideas about 'development' into practical effect. His short book *An Apology for the Revival of Christian Architecture in England*, published in 1843, argued that Gothic needed to be adapted to serve modern needs: 'Any modern invention which conduces to comfort, cleanliness, or durability, should be adopted by the consistent architect; to copy a thing merely because it is old, is just as absurd as the imitations of the modern pagans.'[21] This was of course directly contrary to his teachings in not only *Contrasts*, of which the second edition had appeared only two years before, but also in *The Present State of Ecclesiastical Architecture in England*, published in the same year as the *Apology*, and for that reason historians have often overlooked this characteristically abrupt change of direction. Pugin touches on the reason for it in the peroration to the *Apology*, where he writes that

Catholicism is so interwoven with every thing sacred, honourable, or glorious in England, that three centuries of puritanism, indifference, and infidelity, have not been able effectually to separate it. It clings to this land, and developes itself from time to time, as the better feelings of a naturally honourable man who had been betrayed into sin.[22]

This explicit reference to ideas of development suggests that Pugin was aware of the traditions in Roman Catholic thought that so influenced Newman, but it is possible also that his change of direction may have been influenced by the debates within the OSPGA. Freeman delivered his lecture to the society in March 1843, while Pugin – always quick to absorb new ideas – was working on the proofs of the *Apology*. There can, however, be no question that it was Pugin's own genius that enabled him to give immediate visual shape to the concept of 'developed' Gothic, in the form of the illustrations in the *Apology* of what a Gothic railway station and bridge should look like.[23] In their radically weighty sculptural simplicity, these designs are impressively accurate predictions of the direction that architecture would take in the next decade. Pugin was soon giving this aesthetic concrete form, notably in the bold geometry of St Mary, Rugby, designed in 1845, and in particular its blunt saddle-backed tower. If Pugin, whose practice was by then in decline, had designed many more churches in this manner, his status as a proto-High Victorian would be assured. As Rosemary Hill has argued, he was almost certainly led in the direction of 'development' by his experimental approach to domestic design, where the need to adapt Gothic precedents to suit modern needs was especially pronounced.[24]

Following Pugin, other significant architects in the creation of 'developed' Gothic were drawn into the orbit of the OSPGA. G.G. Scott, who had made his first professional appearance in Oxford in 1840 with his design for the Martyrs' Memorial, was elected a member of the society at the very meeting at which Freeman delivered his lecture on development. There seems little doubt that Scott and Freeman discussed the idea, for in his description of his winning design for the Nikolaikirche competition, written in 1844, Scott uses the term for the first time, although it is confined simply to describing the changing styles of medieval architecture, not to any idea of a new style.[25] William Butterfield's involvement with the OSPGA began in 1843. The following year the society published his drawings of St John, Shotesbrooke, Berkshire, and in 1846 commissioned his restoration of Dorchester Abbey church.

Nonetheless, the OSPGA was not itself responsible either for formulating the conceptual basis of what was to become the High Victorian style, nor did it provide an important forum for deciding the physical form that the style would take. Freeman himself assumed that contemporary architects would either simply take up Gothic again at the point where it had been abandoned in the 16th century or would select an appropriate style for modern times (he favoured Romanesque). There was to be a far more creative response to his concept of architectural development, but it came instead from the Cambridge Camden

Figs.2 & 3 | 'Railway Bridges on the Antient Principles', from A.W.N. Pugin, *An Apology for the Revival of Christian Architecture in England* (1843), in which Pugin first articulated the idea that Gothic should be developed into a modern style. His proposals for Gothic railway bridges are a perceptive forecast of the forms of High Victorian architecture as they were to crystallise in the following decade

Fig.4 | The Flaxman Room, Duchess Street, by Thomas Hope, *c.* 1800. Hope's emphasis on architecture as symbolic form, here exemplified in a room that combined art, ornament and colour on the theme of daybreak, may – thanks to his son – have influenced the High Victorian quest for a form of Gothic that could function as a symbolic language conveying religious meaning

Society, refounded as the Ecclesiological Society when it moved to London in 1846, after the controversy it provoked had forced it out of Cambridge.[26]

Although the Ecclesiological Society occupies a celebrated place in the history of the Gothic revival in England, its very success in imposing its ideas on the architectural profession in the early 1840s has perhaps led to an underestimation of its crucial role in the new direction that the Gothic revival took in the late 1840s. It is not often appreciated that the primacy of 'Middle Pointed' as the ideal model for contemporary architects was overthrown largely by the very society that had set up that paradigm in the first place. In November 1845 Freeman reiterated many of his 1843 arguments in another lecture to the OSPGA, 'Development of Roman and Gothic Architecture, and their Moral and Symbolical Teaching':

> *If Architecture, the first of arts, if Ecclesiastical Architecture, that art applied to the highest ends, if Gothick Architecture, its noblest form, be something more than a stock of details for antiquarian research, or of picturesque effects for the pencil, or of mere aestheticks in any shape, we must look on its successive changes not as a result of mere chance, or of the caprice or taste of individual architects, but as the developments of some great philosophical and moral principles, intimately connected with the spirit and feelings of the successive ages in which they arose.*[27]

This was a decisive occasion because for the first time the ideas about development nurtured by the OSPGA had an impact on A.J.B. Beresford Hope, whom Freeman had first met at the annual meeting of the Archaeological Institute in Winchester in September 1845. The youngest son of Thomas Hope, Beresford Hope (having inherited a fortune from his stepfather) had entered parliament as a Conservative, but was in his own words 'liberal and unshackled by party'.[28] His great interest was ecclesiastical architecture; he had joined the Cambridge Camden Society in 1840 and in 1845 became its chairman. He masterminded not only its change of name the following year, and move to London, but also its subsequent ideological transformation. In March 1846 he wrote to Freeman, 'Christian architecture must be developed to suit present exigencies ... [hence our support for] the principle of development.'[29]

The change was announced in the form of a pair of articles that he published in successive issues of *The Ecclesiologist* in early 1846, articles that condemned the past and pointed the way to the future. The first, 'The Artistic Merit of Mr Pugin', a review principally of Pugin's *The Present State of Ecclesiastical Architecture*, was a withering attack on what Hope declared was Pugin's inability to advance: 'he has not realised that highest standard of Christian art which we expected from him; he has not improved in the degree which we should have hoped for, while all about him were in breathless progress'.[30] This overlooked the recent changes that had taken place in Pugin's architecture, and his declaration of his changing philosophy in the *Apology*, but even if Hope were aware of this, he may perhaps have decided to use Pugin as a target on the grounds that it would have been undiplomatic directly to attack fellow members of the society.

In the following issue, in an article preceding a resumé of Freeman's recent lecture to the OSPGA, disappointment with Pugin was implicitly contrasted with hope for the future. That future was summed up in a single word – 'development'.[31] At this point, however, Beresford Hope proposed an idea of his own. He agreed with the ecclesiologists that modern architects should take Gothic as their foundation, but he argued that they should synthesise a range of sources rather than simply reproducing any single variety of medieval architecture. He did not attack the study of medieval architecture – indeed, the thrust of his criticism of Pugin was Pugin's supposed lack of archaeological discipline – but he wanted to broaden that study:

> *it is something like attempting to limit the power of Omnipotence, to be afraid of looking forward to boundless improvements and developement* [sic]. *Pointed cathedrals may hereafter be built, most truly Pointed, containing all the elements of those already existing, but in so matured a state that Cologne may then become what now we hold Torcello, a curious and venerable remnant of bygone art ... To take the lowest ground we can, do not the achievements of modern science, do not our increased acquaintance with the products of all lands, their marbles, their woods, their ornamental work; do not our increased means of commerce all point to fresh stores of artistical wealth, which may hereafter be devoted to the services of the sanctuary. Christian Architecture has not yet incorporated them, but is Christian Architecture to be tied by a statute of mortmain?*[32]

The Ecclesiological Society had always encouraged both the study of foreign Gothic architecture and of forms of Gothic earlier or later than the Middle Pointed style that they held up as an ideal, but they had not previously welcomed the idea that such studies might provide stylistic models for contemporary design: as one reviewer wrote in the pages of *The Ecclesiologist* in 1846, the society waged an 'enduring war against eclecticism'.[33] However, by that it was meant not eclecticism in the use of sources in a single building, but the use of different styles for different buildings or building types: the ecclesiologists wanted an accepted single style applicable to all buildings. Hope agreed, but he proposed an alternative to archaeological Middle Pointed, namely a new synthetic style.

This idea was Hope's contribution: Freeman's discussion of development had not been meant to encourage stylistic synthesis, and he strongly disliked the way that Hope's idea was translated into practice in High Victorian architecture, especially in Butterfield's buildings.[34] Historians have underrated Hope's most obvious source for his vision of a new Gothic style, although he frequently mentioned it: his father. As an avant-garde designer of furniture and interiors, Thomas Hope had created a personal synthesis of Greek, Egyptian and near-Eastern cultures that was in essence as much Picturesque as archaeological. As an architectural patron as well as a historian he encouraged an equally sophisticated eclecticism. In his country house, Deepdene in Surrey, he drew on Greek, Romanesque and Italian vernacular sources with great fluency, and in his *Historical Essay on*

Architecture, of which the standard two-volume edition was published posthumously in 1835, he gave as much attention to Early Christian, Romanesque and Italian Gothic buildings as he did to classical antiquity.[35]

The book clearly embodies the stylistic eclecticism of the early nineteenth century; less often noted is the way that, thanks to his son, it forms a link with the High Victorian generation, who sought to emulate not merely Hope's knowledge of a wide range of styles but also the way that he proposed synthesising styles into an essentially modern idiom:

> *No one seems yet to have conceived the smallest wish or idea of only borrowing of every former style of architecture, whatever it might present of useful or ornamental, of scientific or tasteful; of adding thereto whatever other new dispositions or forms might afford conveniences or elegancies not yet possessed; of making the new discoveries, the new conquests, of natural productions unknown to former ages, the models of new imitations more beautiful and more varied; and thus of composing an architecture which, born in our own country, grown on our soil, and in harmony with our climate, institutions, and habits, at once elegant, appropriate, and original, should truly deserve the appellation of 'Our Own'.*[36]

These words clearly prefigure his son's arguments a decade later.[37]Beresford Hope objected to the way that the stylistic enthusiasms that emerged in the late 1840s and early 1850s were assumed to be novel: in 1858 he wrote to Freeman that 'I beg to repudiate [the adjective] "Ruskinian" ... my father had written [on] Italian Gothic while Ruskin was still in the nursery.'[38] However, neither Beresford Hope nor Ruskin was the first to propose foreign sources for modern church design; although such major buildings as T.H. Wyatt's and David Brandon's St Mary, Wilton, Wiltshire (1840–46) and J.W. Wild's Christ Church, Streatham, London (1840–42) were in essence one-offs, without progeny, they clearly reveal that many of the elements regarded as characteristic of High Victorian design – notably synthesis of sources and structural polychromy – were not unique to it, and had similar origins in the experimentation and eclectic antiquarian curiosity of Thomas Hope's generation.[39]

Hope could not alone have achieved the practical realisation of his ideals within an ecclesiological Gothic context. His two allies were Benjamin Webb and William Butterfield: the former provided both vital support for Hope's ideas within the Ecclesiological Society and antiquarian expertise in foreign architecture of the sort that Hope did not possess; the second demonstrated in actual buildings how such ideas might be translated into architecture of a high order. Webb, a close friend of Hope at Cambridge, was a clergyman who brought to the Ecclesiological Society the authority of being one of its founders; he was also editor of *The Ecclesiologist*.[40] Unlike the society's other founder, J.M. Neale, who resisted unsuccessfully Hope and Webb's determination to move the society away from its anglophile antiquarianism, Webb studied foreign architecture and took a greater interest than Neale in the development argument, partly because he could see its practical application to a challenge that medieval architects had not had to face: the design of churches for the tropical possessions of the British Empire, a subject on which he published a paper in 1845.[41] Neale realised that the tide was going against him, as he wrote to Webb in December 1846: 'I have grieved, as you know, in almost every number of the *Ecclesiologist* at the enormous space devoted to foreign art ... Do you really suppose that nine-tenths of our subscribers care one straw for our foreign matter? or that a country Priest, wanting real practical information, will endure to be put off with Cologne and Paris? ... I shall not write to Hope: for to make him see where the strength of the *Ecclesiologist* lies would be impossible'.[42]

In 1846 Hope's success would not yet have seemed evident to anyone outside the inner circle of the Ecclesiological Society, but events went his way from then on. One significant embodiment of the new direction the society took under his guidance was the publication in 1848 of Webb's *Sketches of Continental Ecclesiology: Or Church Notes in Belgium, Germany, and Italy*, based on a tour taken in 1845–6. The sketches Webb had made to illustrate it were redrawn for publication by Butterfield. In the first half of the 1840s Butterfield assumed virtually the role of in-house designer for the Ecclesiological Society, to which he had been elected in 1844 – perhaps significantly, at the same meeting at which Hope was co-opted to the committee – a year after he had begun to supply drawings for its books of model designs, the *Instrumenta Ecclesiastica*. In 1844 he begun work on a major commission that he won through Hope's support, St Augustine's College, Canterbury, and by 1845 he had also designed fittings for Hope's estate church at Kilndown, Kent. In addition, as Webb's diary records, in January 1844 Butterfield met Pugin, probably for the first time, and he was quick to absorb the lessons of the Grange at Ramsgate in his own houses.[43] Butterfield was therefore in touch with all the sources of development theory.

In this way the intellectual foundations were laid for the creation of the style we now know as High Victorian, which was given its first complete expression in All Saints, Margaret Street, designed by Butterfield in 1849–50 and largely paid for by Hope, one of its patrons.[44] Webb was its publicist, although the impact of his articles on the church was diminished by the long gap between the start of work in 1850 and the opening of the church in 1859.[45] Nonetheless, Webb almost certainly had a significant influence on the way the new style evolved: the Germanic spire of All Saints may suggest that Butterfield's study of foreign models had taken a lead from Webb, and it was Webb who seems most influentially to have identified the potential significance of Ruskin's writings for contemporary architecture; certainly, it was Webb who enthusiastically reviewed *The Seven Lamps of Architecture* (1849) and, only a little less enthusiastically, the first volume of *The Stones of Venice* (1851) in *The Ecclesiologist*.[46] Although the precise nature of the impact of Ruskin's writings on All Saints, Margaret Street remains a subject for debate, the church's element of Italianate colour derived from its building materials suggests – however much Hope denied it – that Ruskin influenced his abrupt realisation that, as he wrote in April 1850, 'constructional polychrome ... is one of the problems, which the revived Pointed architecture of the nineteenth century, enterprising and scientific as it is, will have chiefly to work out, if it means to vindicate its position of being a living and growing style, and not ... a mere pedantic revivalism'.[47] With this slightly mysterious statement, the final element in the High Victorian aesthetic, constructional colour, was added to the ideals of primitivism and synthesis that had shaped it. Is it possible that Beresford Hope's mind was prepared for this idea by, once again, his father's example? Certainly, Thomas Hope made exceptionally subtle use of coloured marbles and stones in his interiors: in the hall at the Deepdene, for example, classical sculptures were set against slabs of marble set into the walls; mirrors set above green marble fireplaces were framed in red marble, and so on.[48]

Beresford Hope's contribution to the creation of the High Victorian style as it emerged at All Saints, Margaret Street, was fundamental. He was the thinker who decisively crystallised the idea that 'developed' Gothic would be a style based on synthesis, and he did so by reaching back to the ideas of his father and the froth of stylistic debate in the 1830s. That debate seemed to have been stilled by the rise of Middle Pointed in the early 1840s and its short-lived hegemony in the hands of Pugin and the ecclesiologists. In that sense, it is arguable that the High Victorian movement, apparently the most quintessentially 'Victorian' style of all, was in fact a late flowering of a Regency project to produce a new style based on a synthesis of the past. Certainly, just as Thomas Hope had converted the pure 'archaeological' Greek revival into a new Picturesque style based on a synthesis of sources, so under Beresford Hope's guidance, the Gothic revival followed a similar path. The analogy can be taken further. David Watkin, who was the first to point out the links between Thomas Hope's architectural theories and mid-Victorian eclecticism, has emphasised that Thomas Hope's new style was designed as a symbolic language, an idea derived from French architectural theory.[49] The interiors of his house in Duchess Street, for example, incorporate Hope's ideas about symbolic iconography. His decorative scheme for the Flaxman Room (the setting for Flaxman's *Aurora and Cephalus*), executed around 1800, used colour – including coloured marble – to reinforce classical mythological imagery depicting daybreak in 'a remarkable neo-classical attempt to suggest that the spirit of antique art is coincidental with that of eternal nature'.[50]

As Professor Watkin remarks, 'the Hope style created a new iconology which would give complete meaning to every detail of the house's arrangements, such as had been experienced before only in the sequence of religious art within a great church'.[51] It is arguable, therefore, that what Beresford Hope wanted for ecclesiastical architecture in the late 1840s went beyond simply a desire for a new stylistic synthesis analogous to his father's. He encouraged in addition a style that was similarly symbolically dense and semantically loaded. There can surely be no doubt that in the hands of Butterfield, Street, G.F. Bodley and their peers that is precisely what was achieved. In their churches of the 1850s, the use of coloured marble and other stones and ornament derived from the natural world draws on scientific ideas about development to reinforce the message embodied in the iconography of the sculpture and stained glass: the unfolding development of God's plan for his creation. For the space of little more than a decade the High Victorian movement realised with extraordinary intensity architecture's potential as a symbolic and narrative language as understood by Thomas Hope and his son.

NOTES

1. John Summerson, *Architecture in Britain 1530–1830*, 7th ed., Harmondsworth, 1983; Howard Colvin, *A Biographical Dictionary of British Architects 1600–1840*, 4th ed., New Haven and London, 2008; Rupert Gunnis, *Dictionary of British Sculptors 1660–1851*, rev. ed., London, n.d. (1st ed., 1951; new ed. in preparation); Geoffrey Beard and Christopher Gilbert (eds), *Dictionary of English Furniture Makers 1660–1840*, Leeds, 1986; Ian C. Bristow, *Architectural Colour in British Interiors 1615–1840* and *Interior House-Painting Colours and Technology 1615–1840*, both New Haven and London, 1996.

2. Colvin, op. cit. [note 1 above], p. 99.

3. Peter B. Nockles, *The Oxford Movement in Context: Anglican High Churchmanship 1760–1857*, Oxford, 1994.

4. Simon Bradley, 'The Roots of Ecclesiology: Late Hanoverian Attitudes to Medieval Churches', in Christopher Webster and John Elliott, *'A Church as It Should Be': The Cambridge Camden Society and Its Influence*, Stamford, 2000, pp. 22–45.

5. Rosemary Hill, 'Reformation to Millennium: Pugin's Contrasts in the History of English Thought', *Journal of the Society of Architectural Historians*, vol. 58, no. 1 (March 1999), pp. 26–41.

6. Kenneth Clark, *The Gothic Revival*, London, 1928.

7. Michael Hall, 'Introduction', in Michael Hall (ed.), *Gothic Architecture and its Meanings*, Reading, 2002, pp. 6–24.

8. On Hope generally, see David Watkin and Philip Hewat-Jaboor, *Thomas Hope: Regency Designer*, exh. cat., Victoria and Albert Museum, London, and Bard Graduate Center, New York, New Haven and London, 2008. David Watkin, *Thomas Hope and the Neo-Classical Ideal, London*, 1968, discusses the 20th-century revival of Hope at pp. 257–58, a subject that is illustrated by John Martin Robinson in *The Regency Country House: From the Archives of Country Life*, London, 2005, pp. 24–29.

9. Paul Thompson, *William Butterfield*, London, 1971; Stefan Muthesius, *The High Victorian Movement in Architecture 1850–1870*, London, 1972.

10. See G.E. Street's discussion of the links between Pre-Raphaelite art and architecture in 'On the Future of Art in England', *The Ecclesiologist*, vol. 19 (1858), pp. 232–40.

11. W.A. Pantin, 'The Oxford Architectural and Historical Society, 1839–1939', *Oxoniensa*, vol. 4 (1939), pp. 174–79; its connections with Tractarianism are examined in S.L. Ollard, The Oxford Architectural and Historical Society, and the Oxford Movement', *Oxoniensa*, vol. 5 (1940), pp. 146–60.

12. Owen Chadwick, *From Bossuet to Newman: The Idea of Doctrinal Development*, Cambridge, 1957.

13. David B. Brownlee, 'The First High Victorians: British Architectural Theory in the 1840s', *Architectura*, vol. 15 (1985), pp. 33–46.

14. J.H. Newman to Ambrose Phillipps, June 15, 1848, in C.S. Dessain (ed.), *The Letters and Diaries of John Henry Newman*, vol. XII, London, 1962, p. 221.

15. *Proceedings of the Oxford Society for Promoting the Study of Gothic Architecture*, Lent term, 1843, meeting of March 22.

16. James A. Secord, *Victorian Sensation: The Extraordinary Publication, Reception, and Secret Authorship of 'Vestiges of the Natural History of Creation'*, Chicago, 2000. For the possible influence of Chambers's book on architectural thought, see Michael Hall, 'What Do Victorian Churches Mean? Symbolism and Sacramentalism in Anglican Church Architecture 1850–1870', *Journal of the Society*

of Architectural Historians, vol. 49, no. 1 (March 2000), pp. 78–95.
17. Robert Chambers, *Vestiges of the Natural History of Creation*, 2nd ed., London, 1844, p. 362
18. Secord, op. cit. [note 16 above], pp. 256–57.
19. See Hall, op. cit. [note 16 above] and the bibliography cited therein. The history of the Oxford Museum is set out with great thoroughness in Frederick O'Dwyer, *The Architecture of Deane & Woodward*, Cork, 1997, pp. 152–283.
20. A.W.N. Pugin to J.R. Bloxam, September 7, 1840, in Margaret Belcher (ed.), *The Collected Letters of A.W.N. Pugin*, vol. 1 (1830–1842), Oxford, 2001, pp. 140–41.
21. A. Welby Pugin, *An Apology for the Revival of Christian Architecture in England*, London, 1843, p. 8.
22. Ibid., p. 50. On Pugin's change of direction in 1843, see Rosemary Hill, 'Pugin and Ruskin', in Rebecca Daniels and Geoff Brandwood (eds), *Ruskin & Architecture*, Reading, 2003, pp. 221–45, at p. 235.
23. A.W.N. Pugin, op. cit. [note 21 above], Plate III, opposite p. 10.
24. Rosemary Hill, 'Pugin's Small Houses', *Architectural History*, vol. 46 (2003), pp. 147–74; the issue of Pugin and development is discussed further in Rosemary Hill, 'Pugin's Churches', *Architectural History*, vol. 49 (2006), pp. 179–205. I am most grateful to Rosemary Hill for discussing this previously unnoted aspect of Pugin's architectural career with me.
25. Gavin Stamp (ed.), *Personal and Professional Recollections by Sir George Gilbert Scott*, Stamford, 1995, p. 124.
26. The standard history of the society is James F. White, *The Cambridge Movement: The Ecclesiologists and the Gothic Revival*, Cambridge, 1962.
27. *Proceedings of the Oxford Society for Promoting the Study of Gothic Architecture*, Michaelmas Term, 1845, p. 24.
28. Quoted by J. Mordaunt Crook, in *The Oxford Dictionary of National Biography*, q.v. A.J. B. Beresford Hope. See also the very full account of Beresford Hope's career and influence in J. Mordaunt Crook, 'Progressive Eclecticism: The Case of Beresford Hope', in *The Architect's Secret: Victorian Critics and the Image of Gravity*, London, 2003, pp. 85–120, which, however, does not discuss the significance of the term 'development'.
29. A.J. B. Beresford Hope to E.A. Freeman, March 5, 1846. Freeman papers, Rylands Library, Manchester, FA1/1/38a, quoted in J. Mordaunt Crook, *The Architect's Secret*, op. cit. [note 28 above], p. 180, n. 49.
30. Anon. [A.J. Beresford Hope], 'The Artistic Merit of Mr. Pugin', *The Ecclesiologist*, vol. 5 (1846), pp. 10–16, at pp. 10–11.
31. Anon. [A.J. B. Beresford Hope], 'Past and Future Developements of Architecture', *The Ecclesiologist*, vol. 5 (1846), pp. 48–53.
32. Ibid., p. 52.
33. Anon., 'The Church of S. Mary and S. Nicholas, Wilton', *The Ecclesiologist*, vol. 6 (1846), pp. 169–174, at p. 169.
34. See especially Freeman's attack on Butterfield's St Matthias, Stoke Newington, in *The Ecclesiologist*, vol. 11 (1850), p. 209.
35. On the Deepdene, see David Watkin (1968), op. cit. [note 8 above], pp. 158–92.
36. Thomas Hope, *An Historical Essay on Architecture*, 3rd. ed, London, 1840, vol. 1, p. 492.
37. As is observed without discussion by J. Mordaunt Crook, *The Architect's Secret*, op. cit. [note 28 above], p. 105.
38. A.J. B. Beresford Hope to E. A. Freeman, December 29, 1858, Freeman papers, John Rylands Library, Manchester, F1/1/55, quoted in J. Mordaunt Crook, *The Architect's Secret*, op. cit. [note 28 above], p. 90.
39. See Neil Jackson, 'Christ Church, Streatham, and the Rise of Constructional Polychromy', *Architectural History*, vol. 43 (2000), pp. 219–252.
40. On Webb, see J. Mordaunt Crook, 'The Reality of Brick: William Butterfield and Benjamin Webb', in *The Architect's Secret*, op. cit. [note 28 above], pp. 35–84.
41. Benjamin Webb, 'On Pointed Architecture as Adapted to Tropical Climes', *Transactions of the Ecclesiological Society*, 1845, pp. 199–218.
42. J.M. Neale to Benjamin Webb, 12 December 1846, in M.S. Lawson (ed.), *The Letters of John Mason Neale*, London, 1910, p. 100.
43. Benjamin Webb, diary, Bodleian Library,

MS Eng. Misc. e406, 54v, quoted in Rosemary Hill, 'Pugin's Churches', op. cit. [note 24 above], p. 191. As Rosemary Hill points out in 'Pugin's Small Houses', op.cit. [note 24 above], p. 160, the way that Butterfield integrated All Saints, Margaret Street and its parochial buildings onto a square site almost certainly owes a debt to Pugin's Bishop's House in Birmingham (1840–41).
44. Paul Thompson, op. cit. [note 9 above]; see also Paul Thompson, 'All Saints' Church, Margaret Street, Reconsidered', *Architectural History*, vol. 8 (1965), pp. 73–94.
45. Anon. [Benjamin Webb], 'All Saints, Margaret Street', *The Ecclesiologist*, vol. 20 (1859), pp. 184–89, and *The Saturday Review*, vol. 7 (1859), pp. 680–82.
46. Anon. [Benjamin Webb], 'Mr. Ruskin's Seven Lamps of Architecture', *The Ecclesiologist*, vol. 10 (1850), pp. 111–20, and 'Ruskin's *Stones of Venice*', *The Ecclesiologist*, vol. 12 (1851), pp. 275–84 and 341–50.
47. Anon. [A.J. B. Beresford Hope], 'Mr Pugin and *The Rambler*', *The Ecclesiologist*, vol. 10 (1850), pp. 393–99, at p. 398
48. David Watkin (1968), op. cit. [note 8 above], pp. 176–77. The author also draws attention to the continuity of a family interest in marbles in the additions made by Thomas Hope's heir, Henry Hope, to the Deepdene in the 1830s, which included mosaic pavements designed to show off rare marbles, op. cit., p. 182.
49. David Watkin (1968), op. cit.[note 8 above], pp. 193 and 214.
50. David Watkin (1968), op. cit.[note 8 above], p. 113.
51. David Watkin (1968), op. cit.[note 8 above], p. 195. The author reproduces at p. 189 (Fig. 21), an undated sketch design by Beresford Hope for a country house, Erwood in Cheshire, that combines a Picturesque house in the manner of the Deepdene with an apsed chapel in the High Victorian style.

B. The outer surface of the Dome is to be battened with Battens 2½ inches wide & inch thick placed vertically upon which the featheredged boarding is to be laid the same way to form the lips for the lead between the ornaments &c. The extra thickness of the Ribs is to be made out by layers of Battens upon each other breaking joints.

N.B. The lead of Stone below is here omitted to shew the connection of the Section with the Dome. The lead is left with a line to signify that the masonry [illegible] downwards.

No. 180. Patent light skylights to be fixed in the [illegible] of the [illegible] to each rib to vary from 5 in. diameter to 4½ inches diameter around the Dome.

The ribs 6.5 strapped into the stonework at the feet, and to be placed not more than 15 inches asunder at any point on the [illegible]. The ribs to be formed of three thicknesses of inch boarding strongly nailed together with ¾ inch bolts with washers nuts &c to each rib.

36 feet whole diameter of the middle of the Dome

Plan of one quarter of the Dome shewing the abutments

Plan of one quarter of the outer surface of the Dome

Half Elevation & Section of the [illegible] Dome. Drawn to a larger scale

5 · Architectural drawings of the 1840s: a newly discovered portfolio

HELEN DUNSTAN-SMITH AND ROSEMARY HILL

This collection of drawings offers a series of glimpses into the architectural practice of the late Georgian and early Victorian years. The portfolio includes work by Philip Hardwick, William Wilkins, Charles Barry and T. H. Wyatt and his partner David Brandon. The history of the collection is unknown before its recent acquisition by the London dealers Haslam and Whiteway, but it seems likely that it was accumulated in the offices of Wyatt and Brandon, who set up in practice together in Great Russell Street, London, in 1839.

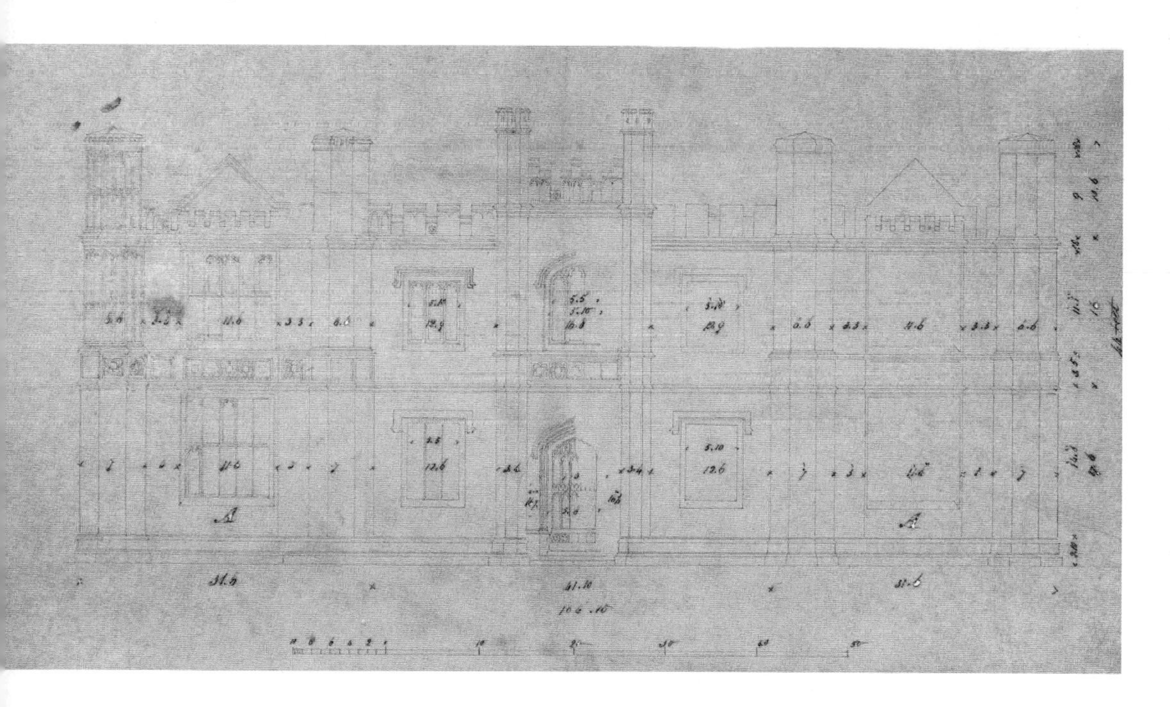

Fig.1 | OFFICE OF WILLIAM WILKINS *Plan, elevation and section of the Great Dome, University College, London,* 60.96 × 43.18 cm. Wilkins belonged to last generation of Georgian architects. A protagonist of the Greek Revival, architect of the National Gallery and of Downing College, Cambridge, he designed University College, London, in 1827–28.

Fig.2 | OFFICE OF WILLIAM WILKINS *Provost's Lodge (now the Library), King's College, Cambridge, Elevation of the North or Principal front,* 30.48 × 48.26 cm

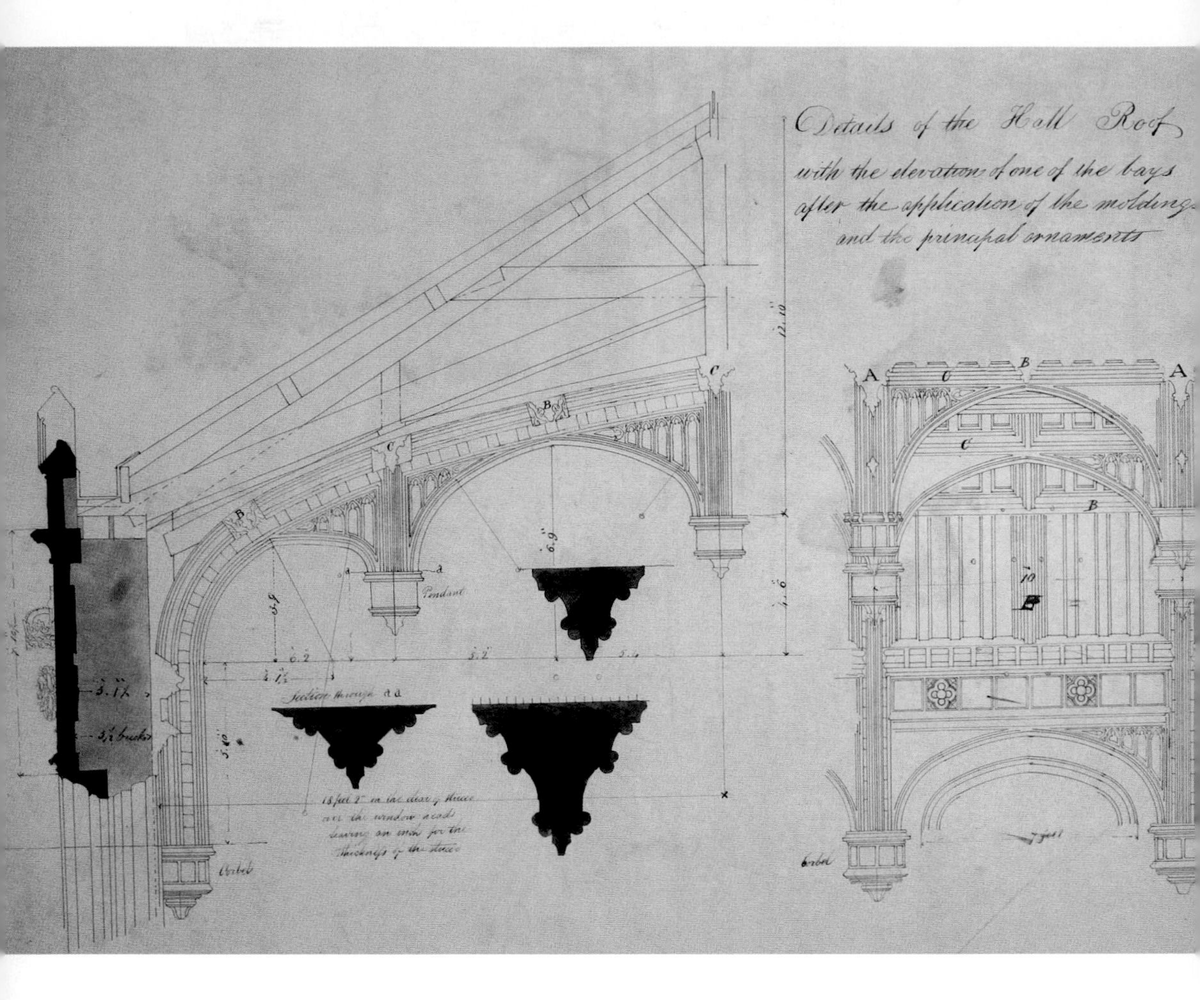

Fig.3 | OFFICE OF WILLIAM WILKINS *King's College, Cambridge, details of the Hall Roof and elevation of one of the bays*, 60.96 × 43.18 cm

Wilkins's Gothic, the sort of design that enraged Pugin and his contemporaries in the 1840s, was in fact more than competent and his work at King's was much admired, especially the screen on King's Parade, which took its inspiration from the college chapel.

Fig.4 | OFFICE OF CHARLES BARRY *The New Houses of Parliament, River front, Bays and Buttresses*, Drawing No.95, Contract No.3, dated 'Westminster Jan 13th 1841', 72.39 × 45.72 cm

Fig.5 | OFFICE OF CHARLES BARRY *North and South Wing, Oriel Details*, Drawing No.199, Contract No.3, dated Feb 4th, 1842, 74.93 × 48.26 cm

As the Palace of Westminster struggled to rise from its foundations in the early 1840s, Barry's office was modifying and simplifying the competition designs created in 1835 by Barry and A. W. N. Pugin and their subsequent estimate drawings. Contract no 3 was a lump sum contract for the building of the river-front façade, awarded to Grissell and Peto. Details were modified yet again in the course of building.

New Houses of Parliament. Curtain Portions. River Front Bays and Buttresses.
No 95. Contract No 3.
Section through Piers
Section through Window
Elevation

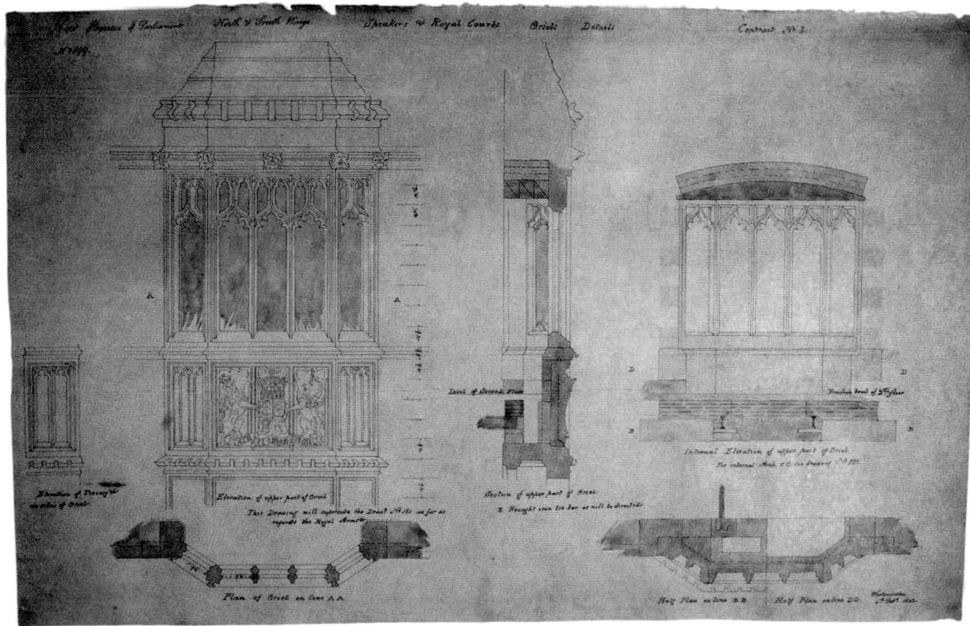
North & South Wings
Speaker's & Royal Courts
Oriel
Details
Contract No 3.
Elevation of upper part of Oriel
Section of upper part of Oriel
Internal Elevation of upper part of Oriel
Plan of Oriel on line A A
Half Plan on line B B
Half Plan on line D D

Reform Club House Upper Library Ceiling enriched Pa
66 3/4
26 in
69 1/8
23 1/4
Centre
58 3/8
34 9/10
Enriched panels.
Additional Molding
to be run round each panel.
Flower in Recess behind Columns in both Libraries.
1/8th Real Size.

th Real Size &c.
48 1/4 in
2 1/4 in
69 1/8
23 5/8
38 1/4 ins
39 1/8 ins
22 1/2 ins
Panels at each end of Room.
Section through beam and Patera Real Size.

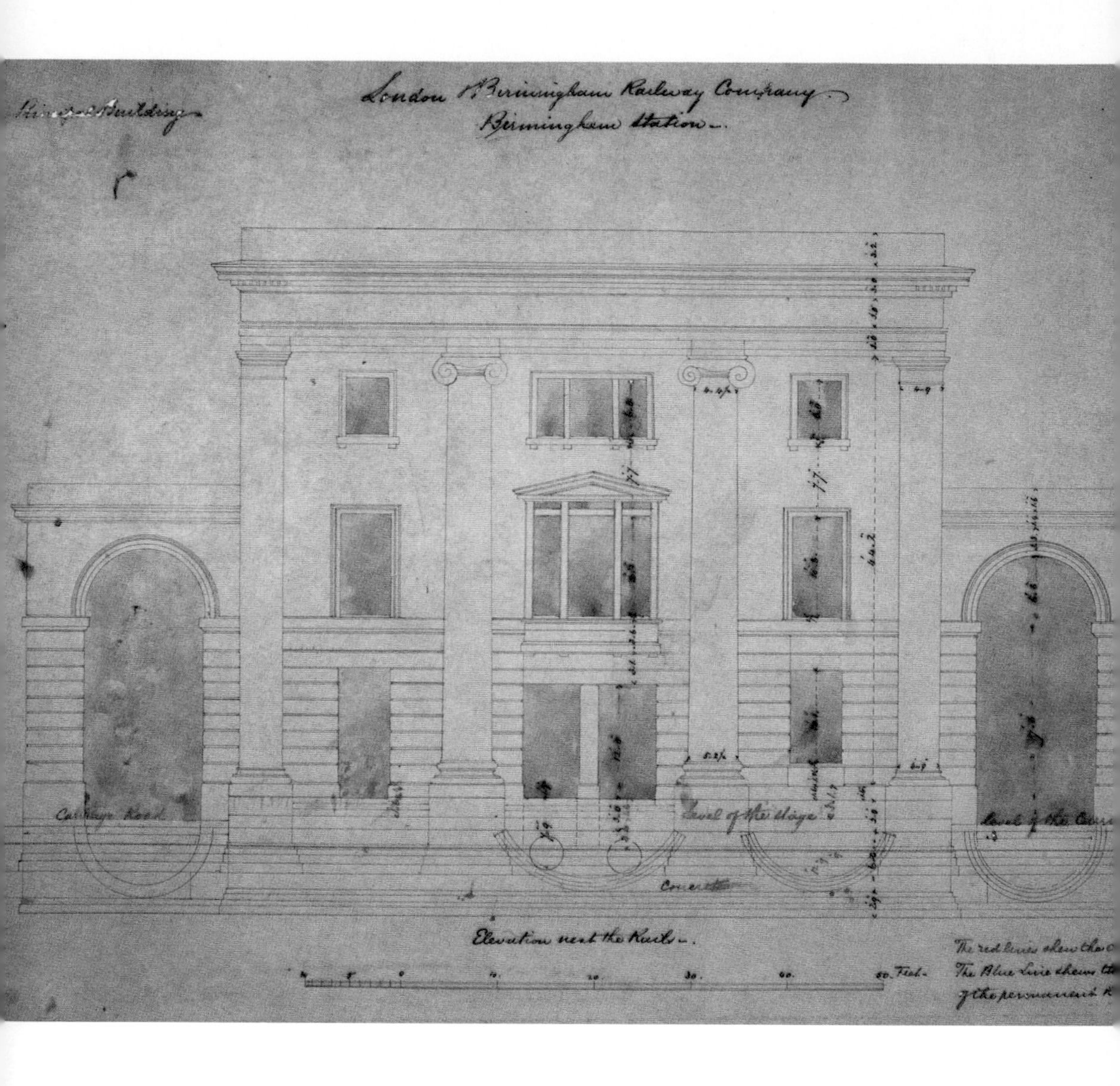

illustrated on pages 80–81
Fig.6 | OFFICE OF CHARLES BARRY
Reform Club, London, Upper Library, ceiling panels, ⅛th real size, 73.66 × 50.8 cm

The Reform Club, in Pall Mall, London, was finished in 1841. Italianate detail of this sort came much more easily to Barry than the Gothic he was required to produce for Westminster.

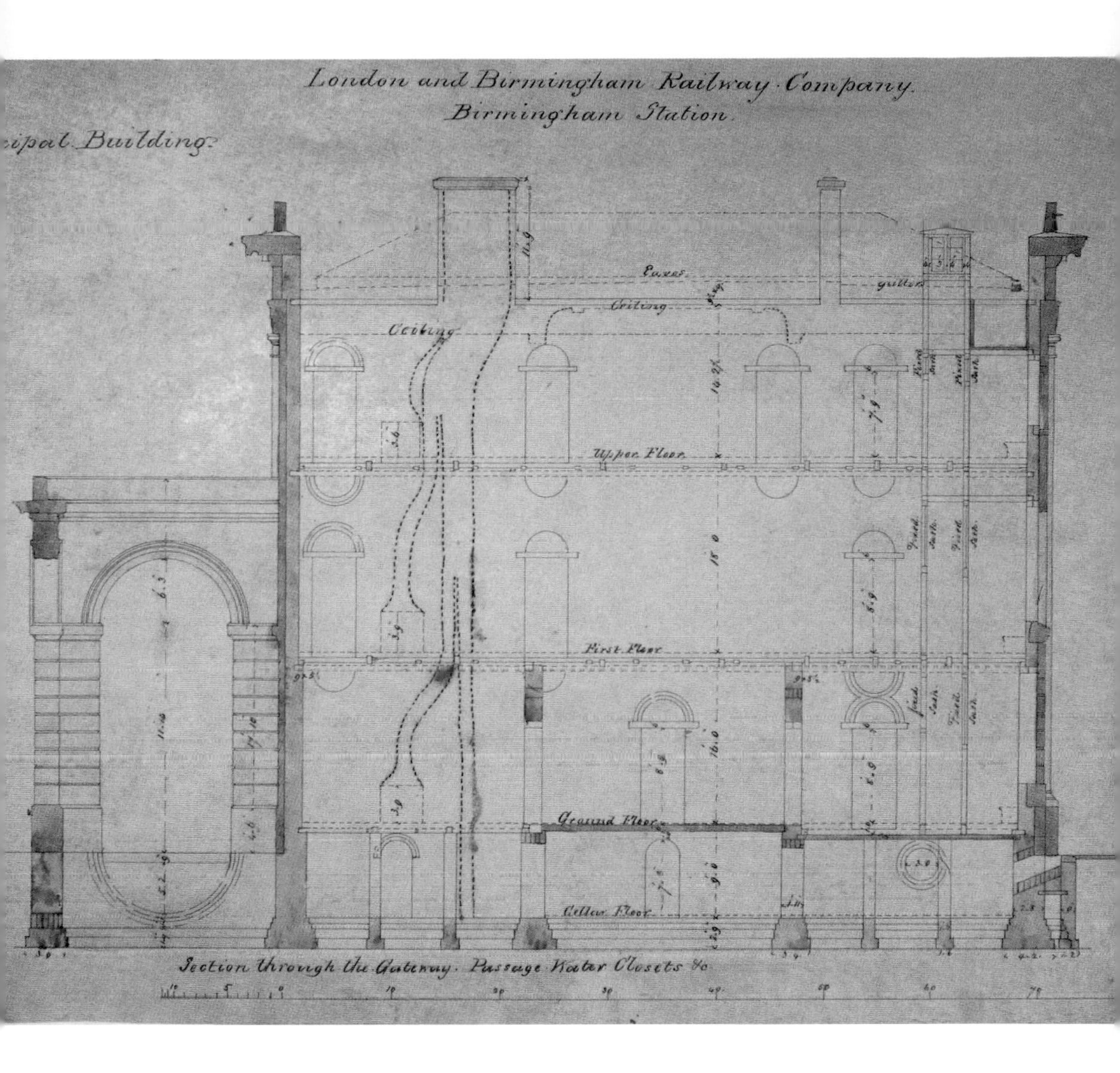

Fig.7 | OFFICE OF PHILIP HARDWICK
Birmingham Station: Section through the gateway, passage and water closets, 35.56 × 45.72 cm

Fig.8 | OFFICE OF PHILIP HARDWICK
Birmingham Station: Principal Building, façade, 38.1 × 45.72 cm

Hardwick was architect to the London and Birmingham Railway Company from 1839 and one of his best-known works was the much-lamented Doric 'Arch' at Euston. His north terminus, to which this drawing relates, was designed and built in 1838–39 and survives, as a fragment, without the wings, in Curzon Street.

Fig.9 | OFFICE OF WYATT AND BRANDON, *Details of the bell turret for St John the Baptist, South Moreton, Berkshire*, 38.1 × 50.8 cm

St John the Baptist is a mostly medieval church heavily restored by Wyatt and Brandon in 1849–50. The bell turret was not built in this form.

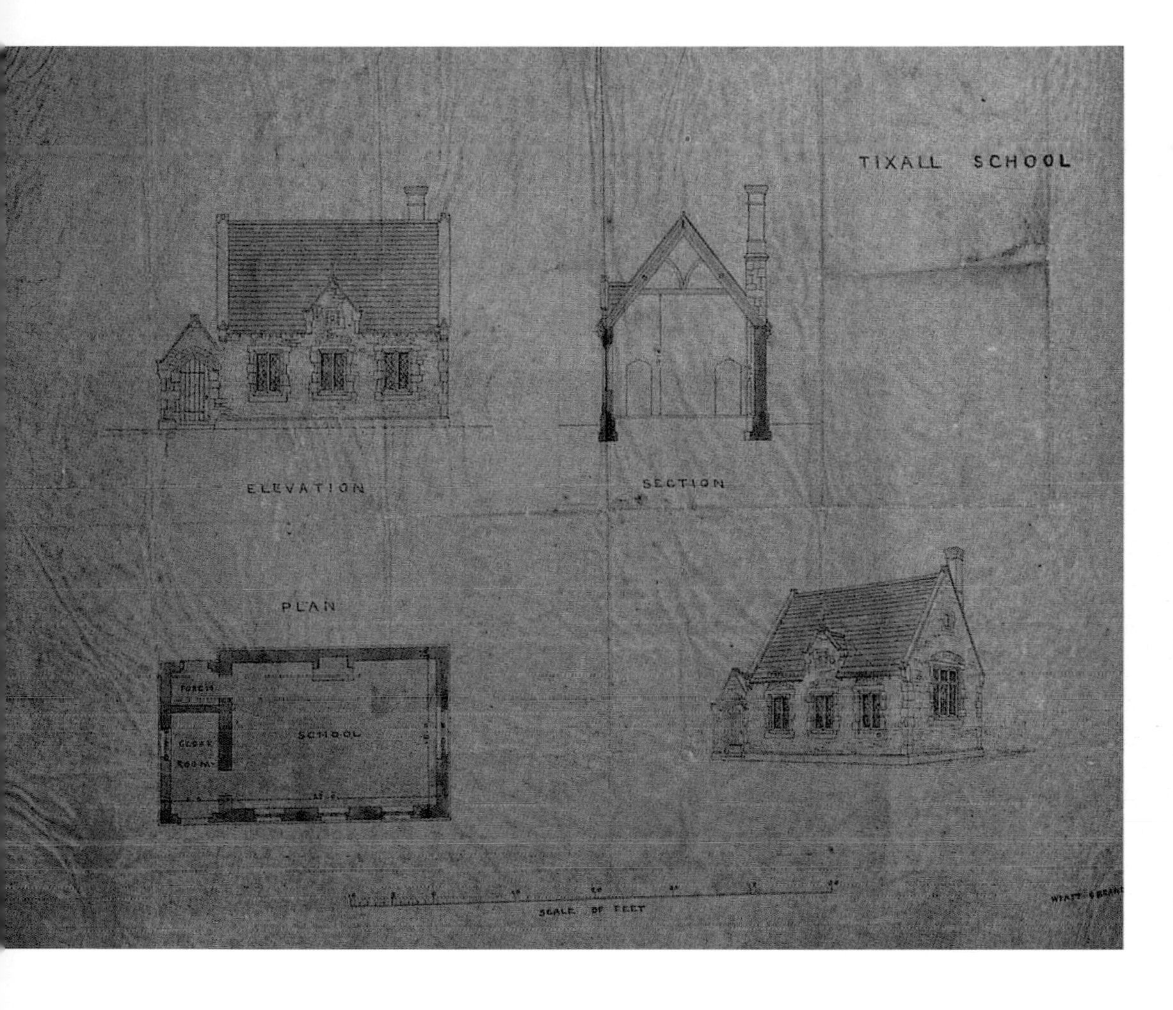

Fig.10 | OFFICE OF WYATT AND BRANDON, *Tixall school, Staffordshire*, elevation, section and plan, 38.1 × 50.8 cm

Land for the school was given by J. C. Talbot, who had employed Wyatt and Brandon to build the village church, St John, in 1849. The school closed early in the 20th century but has now been renovated for use as a village hall.

6 · Elizabeth Simcoe and her daughters: amateur ecclesiastical design in the 1840s

JIM CHESHIRE

Behind the familiar narrative of Victorian church architecture lie many untold and revealing stories, often involving amateurs and women. One such is that of the Simcoes, a Devonshire family of designers.

The story of ecclesiastical architecture and design in the Victorian period has been told many times, but fresh examples resurface periodically that fail to fit in with the narrative. One such example is St Mary, Wreay, in Cumbria designed by a remarkable amateur architect, Sara Losh (Fig.2). In recent years this church has received a considerable amount of attention: two articles, a book and a television series have featured the church since 2000, and Losh is now described as 'architect' by the new *Oxford Dictionary of National Biography*.[1] The attention is justified as the church has both architectural integrity and charm, and the originality of the decorative scheme is undisputed. Although Losh's church is unique in many respects, it should alert scholars of Victorian culture to the potential value of studying amateur ecclesiastical design.

This article will discuss a comparable example, again initiated in the early 1840s and again executed by women. Although perhaps lacking the charm of Losh's work, the activities of Elizabeth Simcoe and her daughters in east Devon raise questions about a narrative of architectural history based exclusively on the activities of the professional.

The work of the Simcoes in the parish of Dunkeswell in east Devon confounds many of our received ideas about the nature of ecclesiastical design in the Victorian period. A hint of what was going on is provided by the *Builder*, which reported in 1846:

> *We cannot avoid making honourable mention of the remarkable perseverance and devotion of the daughters of General Simcoe, who distinguished himself in the American War. These ladies, on the ruins of the old Abbey of Dunkeswell, near Honiton, have erected a church, for which they worked all the stone with their own hands. A large drawing room, commenced by the General, and not finished served for the atelier.*[2]

The photographs illustrating this article are by the author, unless stated otherwise

Fig. 1 | St Nicholas, Dunkeswell, Devon: a corbel depicting Eliza Simcoe by Henry Ezard, *c.* 1868

The Simcoe 'atelier' produced stained glass windows, altars, reredoses, a font, a pulpit, a reading desk, capitals, corbels and furniture reconstituted from antique carvings. This work survives in at least four churches in the Dunkeswell area, and one in Canada. It is likely that all the seven daughters who survived infancy were involved in the enterprise, initially under the direction of their mother. Archival material relating to amateur projects is rare and the fact that it has survived in this case is probably due to the fame of the Simcoe family for other reasons.

Elizabeth Posthuma Simcoe (1762–1850), so named because she was orphaned within hours of birth, is well known to historians as a diarist and artist.[3] Her husband, John Graves Simcoe (1752–1806), made his name in the American War of Independence and was subsequently appointed Lieutenant-Governor of Upper Canada. Elizabeth Simcoe's diaries and paintings of this period, 1791 to 1796, have become a valuable source to Canadian historians. Her adventurous approach to colonial life has appealed to recent commentators to the extent that she has been described as 'one of the most admired founders of modern Ontario'.[4] There is enough evidence to show that both Elizabeth Simcoe and her husband were drawn to romantic medievalism: they both erected Gothic churches on medieval sites within the parish of Dunkeswell and it is known that J. G. Simcoe collected antique armour.[5]

The first of these churches, now known as the 'Wolford Chapel', was built by John Graves Simcoe in 1801 on the site of 'Wulferchurche', a building apparently of Saxon origins that had fallen into disrepair after the dissolution of the monasteries (Fig. 3). This was an estate chapel near Wolford Lodge, the family home, and it is here that most of the family are now buried. The second Simcoe church in the parish was erected in 1842 on the foundations of a Cistercian abbey, a location that Elizabeth Simcoe had been sketching for some time.[6] Her decision to build a church on this site was probably linked with her late husband's belief that he was directly descended from the abbey's founder, Lord William de Brewer. The church, Holy Trinity, was consecrated in 1842, although the interior was not competed until several years later (Fig. 4 and 5). Benjamin Ferrey acted as architect but Elizabeth Simcoe was clearly involved in the design of the church: one of her sketches was described by Sparkes as 'the basis for the plan of the eastern portion of the church'.[7] Between 1838 and 1840, Sir John Kennaway, a family friend of the Simcoes, had built a church on his nearby estate at Escot that has stylistic affinities with Holy Trinity in its severe lancet style and flint masonry.[8] This also suggests that it may have been Elizabeth Simcoe as much as Ferrey who determined the appearance of the building.

In the early 1840s it seems that the Simcoe atelier was working on furnishings for both the Wolford Chapel and Holy Trinity. The carving seems to have come first: the altar and reading desk were in place in Holy Trinity in 1842 (Fig. 5) and an almost identical altar exists in the Wolford Chapel, presumably made at a similar date (Fig. 6). It is likely that the wooden pulpit and capitals at Holy Trinity and the font and pews at the Wolford Chapel were also made at

Fig. 2 | St Mary, Wreay, Cumbria, by Sara Losh, 1842. Photo: Gavin Stamp

Fig. 3 | The Wolford Chapel, Dunkeswell, Devon, rebuilt on the site of 'Wulferchurche' and funded by J. G. Simcoe, 1801

around this time. The atelier's stained- glass production seems to have started after 1842 and was certainly under way in 1844 when a family friend, Hugh Sibbald, visited Wolford Lodge:

> *Sept. 1844. – I was welcomed by Mrs. Simcoe and four daughters – unmarried and of mature age – and after luncheon three of the sisters took me to a long room called the 'workshop,' where they all devote much of their time to carving oak and stone for an ancient church which is being restored on the property. They are now engaged in making a painted window for our Georgina church.*[9]

The 'ancient church' that Sibbald describes was probably the Wolford Chapel, not Holy Trinity as Fryer has assumed, and the window mentioned survives in Canada [explain 'Georgina?] and has distinct stylistic similarities to the east window of Holy Trinity. A further window was installed in a restoration of 1847 in the nearby church St Mary, Hemyock.[10]

Looking at these two interiors in more detail, further intriguing details emerge. That of the Wolford Chapel is quite a puzzle and a thorough examination of the provenance of the furnishings is beyond the scope of this article. The carved wood that dominates the interior consists of material from a variety of dates and locations. The predominant style is late Elizabethan, as seen most impressively in a screen standing against the north wall (Fig. 8).[11] Given J. G. Simcoe's romantic tendencies it is quite possible that some of this woodwork was incorporated into the chapel soon after its rebuilding in 1802, but several pieces of evidence suggest that much of it was installed later, under the influence of Elizabeth Simcoe. We know from Sibbald's diary that stone and oak were being carved for this interior in 1844 – the altar, font and a variety of wooden fragments attached to older carving are evidence of this activity. Although sales of historic carved wood for similar purposes are known to have taken place in the early 19th century, the Welsh character of some of the carving suggests a connection to Elizabeth Simcoe's Welsh ancestry and her picturesque tours of Wales, where she might have acquired antique carvings.[12]

Some of the alterations to the woodwork have affinities to Elizabeth Simcoe's scheme at Holy Trinity, for example the introduction of the arms of the see of Exeter in the screen on the north wall echoes the carving on the west wall of the former church. As the Simcoes' own estate church, this building offered an opportunity for them to experiment, and the comparatively crude nature of some of the carving suggests that this may be some of the earliest work they executed. The box pews, made up from a mixture of antique fragments may have been the work of the Simcoes in the 1840s or they could be older. It is almost certain, however, that the Simcoes did make use of antique wood carvings, a fact suggested by a series of unusual Gothic chancel chairs that exist in buildings associated with the Simcoe atelier. One in Holy Trinity combines the Simcoe arms with older work while a pair at Hemyock has sections which seem to have been taken from the same batch of carving used to make up the pews at the Wolford Chapel (Fig. 7).

Fig. 4 | Holy Trinity, Dunkeswell Abbey, Devon, by Benjamin Ferrey and Elizabeth Simcoe, consecrated 1842

Fig. 5 | Holy Trinity, Dunkeswell Abbey, Devon: the altar and reredos, carved in the Simcoe atelier and in place by 1842

Politically, both Simcoe parents were assertively anti-republican and vigorous supporters of the Church of England: they campaigned hard for the endowment and establishment of the Anglican Church in Canada. These affiliations are not unusual for romantic medievalists, but Elizabeth Simcoe's connection to the Evangelical wing of the Anglican Church is far less typical, although it is possible, as one author suggests, that she moved further towards the Evangelicals after the death of her eldest son and her best friend in 1812–13.[13] She seems to have been connected to the Clapham Sect and was even known to Francis Close, later the archenemy of ecclesiology, whom she and her daughters had probably met during their frequent sojourns at Cheltenham.[14] Her son, Henry Addington Simcoe, became an Evangelical clergyman and theologian, and preached the sermon at the consecration of Holy Trinity, an event that also moved local poet Alfred Dunsford to pen some lines of a decidedly Evangelical tone, if doubtful poetic value:

Where once an Abbey stood – within whose towers
Monks sung their Vesper hymns at midnight hours,
Where superstition held her madd'ning reign,
And wall re-echoed with the Papal strain –
Now stands the Church of God; and on this day
Assembled tribes meet here again to pray,
To hear the Consecration service read,
Within that Church for which our fathers bled.[15]

The building alone presents ample evidence of a Low Church approach. Despite the decoration it is austere, with a plain exterior and a bright interior, aided by the lack of stained glass in the large south facing lancets (Fig. 9). Figures are noticeably absent from the entire decorative scheme, suggesting a characteristic

Fig. 6 | The Wolford Chapel, Dunkeswell Devon: the interior looking east, benches an pews probably made up in the Simcoe atelie

Fig. 7 | St Mary, Hemyock, Devon: chancel chair, probably made up by the Simcoe atelier in the mid 1840s. Notice the left and right borders of the back of the chair, which match other antique carving in the Wolford Chapel

Fig. 8 | The Wolford Chapel, Dunkeswell Devon: font and screen on north wall, late sixteenth century, with alterations and additions, probably by the Simcoe atelier in the early 1840s

Evangelical mistrust of figurative imagery. Attractive medieval tiles discovered during the excavation of the foundations were reset around the fixed stone altar carved by the Simcoes. A few years later, after the controversy over St Sepulchre (the Round Church) at Cambridge, this might have been considered both 'papal' and illegal, but no-one considered it so in 1842,[16] although it was singled out in a brief second-hand description that appeared in the *Ecclesiologist* in 1842:

> *WE hear high accounts of DUNKESWELL Chapel, Somersetshire: it was built by six ladies, the ornamental part being done by their own hands. The Altar is stone, and good; the seats of oak, and well panelled. Some tiles, dug up from Dunkeswell Abbey, are laid down before the Altar. We could wish for a more detailed account.*[17]

The *Ecclesiologist* later acknowledged receiving a further 'interesting account' of the church but offered no further comment: it is doubtful whether they liked what they heard in the more detailed description.[18]

Only Eliza and Caroline Simcoe lived long enough to contribute to the much later restoration of the parish church, St Nicholas, Dunkeswell. They died in 1865 and 1864 respectively and so their contributions must have been planned quite a long time in advance, as the restoration was not completed until 1868. A plaque in the church records that it was planned 'with the aid of Miss Simcoe of Wolford Lodge', suggesting that Eliza had taken on her mother's role of advising the architect. She seems to have retained her mother's Evangelical approach to design, as the stained glass (this time by a professional) is restrained; symbols and patterns adorn the tracery but the main lights remain clear. The retention of the family pew further suggests an attitude unaffected by ecclesiology. Eliza and Caroline Simcoe's carving in the church shows that their skill had developed considerably. Although the reredos is similar in design to that in Holy Trinity, the carving of the miniature capitals is far more sophisticated (Fig. 10). Only one type of foliage was used in the reredos at Holy Trinity, whereas here each of the 18 capitals is different. The carving of the corbels in the chancel and aisles might still be considered slightly heavy alongside that of a professional, but is certainly competent and has a certain vigour that professional work can lack.

In this last project the Simcoes also seem to have acquired a protégé: the zinc panels in the arcade of the reredos were painted with appropriate texts by the daughter of the vicar, the Revd Richard Croly, also a moving force in the restoration. The work of six of the Simcoe daughters is commemorated in St Nicholas

Fig. 9 | Holy Trinity, Dunkeswell Abbey, Devon: the interior looking east. The capitals, corbels and stained glass were produced by the Simcoe atelier in the mid-1840s

Fig. 10 | St Nicholas, Dunkerswell, Devon: the reredos, probably carved by Eliza or Caroline Simcoe in the mid-1860s. The lettering on zinc panels is by the daughter of the Revd Richard Croly

by six corbels in the nave, each carrying the face of one of the Simcoe daughters (Fig. 1) and a plaque in the church commemorates the 'Departed Sisters of Wolford Lodge Whose Memory Hallows the Scene of their Labours'.[19] The seventh daughter, Anne, married a servant after her mother's death and subsequently seems to have been ostracised by the rest of the family. Her omission from the commemoration seems a little unjust, as she was certainly involved in the family's parochial work.

The work of the Simcoes seems to anticipate later 19th-century ideas about the nobility of making. It is likely that the Simcoes conceived their carving and painting as part of a broader spectrum of charitable work, which they were involved in on a number of fronts.[20] This may not be the Art and Crafts Movement but their work is an example of an intricately orchestrated campaign of craft, organised and executed by two generations of women. This campaign did not fit the mould that the men of the Cambridge Camden Society were busily forming at the same time: the Simcoes had a different religious affiliation that they expressed clearly through their interior schemes. Elizabeth Simcoe and her daughters were very wealthy, and because of this could be independent, but their decision to leave a permanent record of their work in a manner that reflected their Evangelical Anglicanism is remarkable. Instead of pursuing the kind of ephemeral craft that women might have been expected to participate in, they chose to construct and ornament permanent architectural fittings, which survive to this day. Given the individual nature of the work it is fascinating that six of the seven daughters chose not to marry and it is tempting to interpret this as statement of independence that parallels their unusual activities in the parish.[21] Further research may reveal more about the gender politics of this example but it is clear that the work of the Simcoes serves to enhance our sense of the richness and diversity of ecclesiastical architecture and design in the 1840s.

Amateur ecclesiastical design deserves to be taken seriously. The artistic merit of amateur work might be debatable but historians of Victorian culture have much to learn from the activities of such people as the Simcoes and Sara Losh. Amateur work in the following decades became more common and was normally closely linked to Camdenian ecclesiology. Despite this, many amateur productions retain an idiosyncrasy, which allows us a glimpse of how certain Victorians participated in their religion in unorthodox ways and underlines the fact that religious activity was not always controlled by the establishment.

NOTES

1. See Rosemary Hill, 'Romantic Affinities', *Crafts*, no. 166 (September/October 2000), pp. 34–39; J. B. Bullen, 'Sara Losh: architect, romantic, mythologist', *The Burlington Magazine*, vol. 143 (November 2001), pp. 676–84. Simon Jenkins featured the church in his television series 'The English Church' broadcast by Channel 4 in 2002 and the related book *England's Thousand Best Churches*, London, 1999.

2. *The Builder*, vol. 4 (1846), p. 533. Elizabeth Simcoe had eight daughters: Eliza (1784–1865), Charlotte (1785–1842), Henrietta Maria

(1787–1845), Caroline (1788–1858), Sophia Jemima (1789–1864), Katherine I (1794–1794), Katherine II (1801–1861) and Anne (1804–1877).

3. Mary Beacock Fryer, *Elizabeth Postuma Simcoe 1762–1850: A Biography*, Toronto, 1989.

4. Mary Lu MacDonald, 'Elizabeth Postuma Simcoe (1762–1850)', *Oxford Dictionary of National Biography*, Oxford, 2004.

5. Fryer, op. cit. [note 1 above], p. 180.

6. The present location of these sketches is unclear. In the 1970s J. A. Sparkes, the author of a subsequent book about the medieval abbey, copied a number of the sketches and attempted speculative reconstructions of certain features, particularly the stained glass. He deposited his copies and reconstructions with the Devon Record Office (DRO: 2331 Z/Z1 & 2331/Z/Z2). Many of these were published in his subsequent history, *In the Shadow of the Blackdowns*, Bradford on Avon, 1978.

7. DRO 2331 Z/Z1–Z2. Ferrey's design for Holy Trinity is currently displayed in the church.

8. The architect for St Philip and St Nicholas, Escot, was Henry Roberts, who had also rebuilt the house for Kennaway, see B. Cherry and N. Pevsner, *Buildings of England, Devon*, 2nd ed., London, 1989, p. 356

9. Quoted in Francis Paget Hett, *Georgina: A Type Study of Early Settlement and Church Building in Upper Canada*, Toronto, 1939. This quotation is included (although abbreviated and slightly misquoted) in Fryer, op. cit. [note 3 above], p. 228

10. St. Mary's Church, Hemyock, Devon was restored in 1846–47 by Richard Carver. Elizabeth Simcoe contributed to the restoration fund and her son preached the sermon at the re-opening: see Fryer, op. cit. [note 1 above], p. 234. The east window of the south aisle is undoubtedly the work of the Simcoe atelier.

11. I am grateful for the opinion of my colleague Dr John Lord on the earlier woodwork.

12. See Clive Wainwright, *The Romantic Interior*, New Haven and London, 1989, pp. 54–60. Fryer records that one such tour took place in 1831: see Fryer, op. cit. [note 3 above], p. 214–15.

13. Macdonald, op. cit. [note 4 above].

14. It is known that Close wrote to the family recommending a mistress for Dunkeswell School: see Fryer, op. cit. [note 3 above], pp. 224–5

15. From 'Lines on the Consecration of a Church Built on the Ruins of Dunkeswell Abbey', printed fragment attached to DRO 2332 Z/Z 1–2. Dunsford was a doctor from Culmstock whose work has been described as containing 'very little of general or real poetic merit': see W. H. K. Wright, *West-Country Poets their Lives and their Works*, London, 1896, pp. 162–63.

16. For an account of the controversy over St Sepulchre, see Chris Miele, 'Re-presenting the church militant: the Camden Society, church restoration, and the Gothic sign', in Christopher Webster and John Elliot (eds), *'A Church as it Should Be' the Cambridge Camden Society and its Influence*, Donnington, 2000, pp. 263–78

17. *The Ecclesiologist*, vol. 2 (1842), p. 58.

18. *The Ecclesiologist*, vol. 2 (1842), p. 111. (No. XVIII, January, 1843) – what does this second ref. refer to?

19. Another plaque on the church commemorates the sculptor of these corbels, Henry Ezard, who died soon after the completion of the restoration.

20. One source states that Eliza, Caroline and Anne had a 'parish' each: Dunkeswell Abbey, Luppit and Dunkeswell, where they delivered and oversaw the education of the parishioners. See J. Ross Robertson, *The Diary of Mrs. John Graves Simcoe*, Toronto, 1911, p. 363.

21. Robertson suggests that Elizabeth Simcoe forbade her daughters to marry, an assertion that seems to have been based on thin evidence and has been sensibly discussed and questioned by Fryer. See Robertson, op. cit. [note 20 above], p. 363 and Fryer, op. cit. [note 3 above], p. 203.

WEAMAN ST.

7 · The Bishop's House, Birmingham

TIMOTHY BRITTAIN-CATLIN

On 20 November 1959 Mark Girouard, a founder member of the Victorian Society and an architectural writer at *Country Life*, visited the Bishop's House in Bath Street, Birmingham, following the decision by the Roman Catholic archdiocese to agree to its demolition by the city council.[1] *Country Life* photographers recorded the building in great detail, but in the end Girouard's proposed article was shelved, and almost none of the photographs have previously been published.

The house that stares out from these striking images was designed by A. W. N. Pugin in late 1840 on the basis of a highly original form of corridor planning that he had been developing since his earlier presbytery, now also demolished, at St Mary, Derby. Although the Bishop's House resembled the northern French *hôtels* that Pugin saw on his travels, the internal layout was quite different. A visitor to the great hall, which is immediately above and to the right of the front door, was required to walk around a narrow spiral route that coiled almost the entire length of all sides of the building. It makes a striking contrast to the planning of Anglican bishops' palaces of the period, with their grand stairs and broad formal routes.

The house had its detractors from the start: Joseph Bowden, president of the seminary at Sedgley Park, near Wolverhampton, Staffordshire, described it as 'the most gloomy place I ever saw'.[2] More fatally, in the 20th century, the diocesan surveyor C. H. Whitehouse told Archbishop Masterson in 1952 that he 'personally [did] not think it worth-while objecting to the proposed removal of Bishop's House'.[3] Moreover, the city engineer Sir Herbert Manzoni seemed determined to pull it down, since he told Masterson's successor, Francis Grimshaw, that it could be saved only if the diocese itself would be prepared to pay for any resulting alteration to his ring road scheme.[4] It had, of course, no money to do so, and it needed the compensation. And thus it came about that one of the most extraordinary buildings in Britain was replaced by a traffic island.

The photographs illustrating this article are all from the *Country Life* Picture Library

Fig. 1 | The southern corner of the Bishop's House in Bath Street, Birmingham, seen from the liturgical west end of St Chad's cathedral. The ornamental stone surround to the entrance door was added after the death of A.W.N. Pugin

Fig. 2 | *previous spread* The entrance front of the house from Shadwell Street, which ran alongside the liturgical north front of the cathedral towards Snow Hill Wharf. The house's great hall is identified by the pointed window, above right

Fig. 3 | A view north down Weaman Street towards St Chad's; the oriel window to the left of the great chimney of the Bishop's House lit the bishop's chamber

Fig. 4 | The great hall on the first floor, dominated by Pugin's characteristic tables and Glastonbury chairs. The latter were based on a surviving medieval original in the Bishop's Palace in Wells

Fig. 5 | The audience chamber at the southern corner of the building, overlooking the great west door to St Chad's

Fig. 6 | The fireplace in the former bishop's chamber. The Bishop's House was so thoroughly recorded by *Country Life*, as well as by others including the Birmingham photographer Logan, that it can be reconstructed in considerable detail

Fig. 7 | The chapel, behind the great hall. What looks here like the underside of the roof, visibl to the left, is an architectural sleight of hand: the real roof rises up towards a party wall, and this is a suspended ceiling that imitates a conventional pitch

Fig. 8 | The great hall was separated fron the final stretch of the long corridor route that weaves it way up through the house by a glazed screen. The chapel wa beyond this corridor

Fig. 9 | The fireplace in the great hall; Bishop Thomas Walsh's initials appear i the spandrels

Fig. 10 | The library, which lay between the chapel and the bishop's chamber on the first floor, and which like the chapel had a misleading suspended ceiling. The clerestory window to the left overlooked the courtyard at the front of the building

NOTES

1. The house was designed at the outset as a 'bishop's' house although it was planned 10 years before the restitution of the Roman Catholic hierarchy in England because its first incumbent, the Vicar Apostolic of the Midland District Thomas Walsh, like all Vicars Apostolic, held a titular see. Walsh was Bishop of Cambysopolis. The see of Birmingham was elevated to the status of archdiocese in 1911.

2. Quoted in E. Buscot, *A History of Cotton College*, London, 1940, p. 154. The remark is undated but Bowden died in 1844.

3. Letter of November 21, 1952, Birmingham Archdiocesan Archives, file P1/44.

4. My gloss, from the minutes of a meeting between the bishop and his advisers and the city engineer and architect on February 8, 1957, ibid.

The photographs illustrating this article are by the author, unless stated otherwise
Fig. 1 | The only known photograph of William White. Undated.
Courtesy of the RIBA Photograph Collection

8 · William White: the early years

GILL HUNTER

William White left Gilbert Scott's office in 1847. In the following three years he was based in Cornwall, producing ecclesiastical, domestic and public buildings that announced the arrival of a major talent.

William White has been described by Mark Girouard as 'one of the most interesting and least known of Victorian Gothic revivalists' (Fig. 1).[1] It is not surprising that so little is known of him, for no personal papers or diaries appear to have survived; nor have records of his architectural practice, which stretched from 1847 until his death in 1900. His practice appears always to have been small, so that, as an obituarist noted, 'like the man of enthusiasm that he was, he relied upon himself alone to do the best he was capable of, trusting to his own common sense, and giving to the workmen the drawings of his own hand, that nothing of his intention might be lost'.[2] The most promising of his pupils, John Ford Gould from Barnstaple, died young and, unlike George Gilbert Scott, White did not leave a family of architects to inherit his practice – his only son, William Holt-White, was a journalist and writer of science fiction who died childless. And although a prolific writer of letters, papers, articles and pamphlets, White published no books to reach a wider public audience. I suspect, too, that his lack of reputation is the fault of 20th-century historical perspective: Henry-Russell Hitchcock concluded that too many critics base their judgement of Victorian architecture on large public buildings, and White did not work in this field.

William White was born at Blakesley, Northamptonshire, on 12 April 1825, the third son of the Revd Francis Henry White. After a home education, William was apprenticed, at the age of 15, to Daniel Goodman Squirhill, an architect and surveyor, of Leamington. Although he was taught, as he described, 'some of the principles of construction, of quantities, and of the supervision of work', he learnt 'little in the way of design or drawing', and had to 'depend greatly for his knowledge on the studies which he followed out on his own account'.[3] An obituary of White described him as 'a conscientious and successful worker in the school of the Gothic Revival, and ... doubted whether in that band of ardent and enthusiastic men there was one who paid more respect to the teachings of Welby Pugin, or who has shown in his work his ability to apply the principles enunciated in that school with greater facility'.[4] As his eldest brother, H. M. White, a Fellow of New College 1839–58, was 'deeply influenced by contact with the leaders of the Oxford

Movement' and was a life member of the Oxford Architectural Society, it seems likely that White would have studied the works of Pugin by the time he joined George Gilbert Scott's practice as an 'improver' in 1845.[5] Also in Scott's office at Spring Gardens were George Frederick Bodley and George Edmund Street, who became his close friends. Scott and Street were both members of the Ecclesiological (formerly Cambridge Camden) Society, which White joined in 1848, a year after he left London to establish his own practice in Truro, Cornwall.

In the 1840s the Exeter diocese (which included Cornwall) under Bishop Henry Philpotts, an early patron of the Cambridge Camden Society, was a centre of the High Church movement. Incumbents of Cornish parishes appointed by Philpotts built and restored churches and established schools in an effort to counter the strong nonconformism of the poor mining and fishing population. The Exeter Diocesan Architectural Society was established under Philpotts' patronage in 1841, the first of such societies outside the two universities. Philpotts had been chaplain to William Van Mildert, Bishop of Durham, a relative of White's mother. Although they had disagreed over Catholic Emancipation, Van Mildert had supported Philpotts' appointment to Exeter, so perhaps White felt he would be favoured in return.

In May 1847 the Revd William Haslam, graduate of the new university that Van Mildert had established in Durham, applied to the Incorporated Church Building Society for aid towards the building of a new church, St Michael, at Baldhu, a mining district approximately 4 miles south-west of Truro, for which plans had been drawn up by William White. The patron, the 2nd Earl of Falmouth, had agreed to pay half of the £1,785 cost, which included £30 for the architect's commission and travelling expenses as well as the salary of a clerk of works.

Built of coursed elvan rubble, St Michael consists of nave and chancel under an unbroken Delabole slate roof, and a gabled south aisle with the entrance porch towards its western end. Due to disuse and years of vandalism prior to being sold for conversion to a dwelling, the church is now boarded up, so that White's tracery in Decorated style cannot be seen. Pale limestone is employed for the moulded doorways and hoodmoulds to the windows, and for the broach spire to the northern tower (Fig. 2). This is typical of White's early work in Cornwall, where local materials offered only the subtlest of external colouring: the sombre grey of the Delabole slates against the silvery stone of the walls and the even paler dressings. In contrast, the interior includes small brightly-coloured patterns on the corbels and evidence of painting on some of the carved floriated capitals. *The Ecclesiologist* reported that 'the chancel, sedilia, and credence are ornamented with trefoil patterns, painted by Mr. Haslam', and that it was intended further to embellish the 'very richly moulded and carved' pulpit (now sadly vandalised; Fig. 3), by decorating the five traceried panels 'with paintings of the Evangelists and S. Michael'.[6] Consecrated on 20 July 1848, the church's stained-glass east window by Beer of Exeter and White's favoured buff, red and black floor tiles would have provided a polychromatic focus for services. Haslam reported that 'The Church

Fig. 2 | The tower and spire, St Michael, Baldhu, Cornwall, 1847–48

Fig. 3 | The pulpit, St Michael, Baldhu, Cornwall, 1847–48

Fig. 4 | St Gerent, Gerrans, Cornwall, from the east. The church was restored by White in 1849–50

Fig. 5 | Pews, St Gerent, Gerrans, Cornwall, 1849–50

is completed in a manner wh. meets the approval and admiration of all who see it.'[7]

On 4 May 1849 *The Royal Cornwall Gazette* reported the laying of the foundation stone for the rebuilding of the parish church at Gerrans (about 7 miles south-east of Truro), which in its dilapidated state had become 'a dishonour to God, and a disgrace to the parish'. Early plans by a Mr Pryor for the rebuilding were superseded, after a fire destroyed the roof, by those of White, 'the talented architect of Baldiu [sic] Church', which the incumbent, another Oxford man, the Revd W. D. Longlands, described as 'much better than those originally sent'.[8] In a statement that presaged his future attitude to restoration, White asserted that 'the Character of the old Church should be preserved as no other proportions would be suitable to the Steeple ... [and] because it contains some peculiarities of style which it would be wrong to destroy' (Fig. 4).[9]

This seems to reflect not only an antiquarian, picturesque aesthetic, but also an appreciation of vernacular style and use of materials that would imbue all his work. White's 'literal rebuilding, the very stones of the almost Debased piers and arches having been replaced, and the old windows, so far as possible, used again' was not approved of by *The Ecclesiologist*, which decided that this 'was an instance where a wholly new church might have been expected'.[10]

Here, White employed a characteristic simple outline – no buttresses or plinth – of slatestone rubble, with granite and freestone dressings, some of which comprise single huge, vertical blocks to form the window jambs. The windows vary, with single lancets in the north wall of the nave, traceried lights to the east end of the chancel and south aisle, and a small perpendicular light that White removed from the north chancel wall and inserted in the east wall of the new vestry, constructed to the north-east of the chancel. Around the head of the traceried two-light window at the west end of the south aisle thin pieces of slatestone have been successfully arranged like voussoirs, without disturbing the flatness of the wall surface.

The interior of the church is equally simple, with plastered walls beneath a trussed rafter roof, fewer rafters at the east end being the only distinction between nave and chancel. Although the rood screen and font cover have now been removed, White's decorative iron altar rail fortunately remains, as do his oak benches with their rolled edges and simple pegged construction – described by Clive Wainwright as 'splendidly plain and solid' – which pre-date William Morris's massive furniture of 1856 onwards (Fig. 5).[11]

White was anxious to apply the Gothic style to secular buildings and was given the opportunity with the demolition of the old Coinage Hall, Truro, which began in May 1848. An obituary of White refers to his 'Bank and Solicitors' Offices, which occupy the site of the old Stannery Court', at the junction of Princes Street and Boscawen Street (Fig. 6). Sensitive, perhaps, to local feeling, which might have condemned a medieval design as too ecclesiastical, White's building for the Cornish Bank is of coursed rubble with granite dressings in Perpendicular style.

Fig. 6 | Bank, Truro, 1848–50, photographed *c.*1902–18. Photo courtesy of Lloyds TSB Archives. The building is currently occupied by Pizza Express

Fig. 7 | The Rectory, St Columb, Cornwall, designed in 1849. Print by Leighton Brothers, from a drawing by William White. Courtesy of the Royal Institution of Cornwall

Fig. 8 | Stained glass, the Rectory, St Columb, Cornwall, 1849–51

Fig. 9 | The stone staircase, the Rectory, St Columb, Cornwall, 1849–51

However, it contains features that would become typical of White: a strong, varied roofline; windows very flat in the wall plane; and what would be recognised as his 'inventive and ingenious' talent, here found in the main doorway, where the two doors hinge back on each other to expose the porch, and in the pivoting windows operated, like those in a greenhouse, by winding handles.[12]

Although White was not listed as a member of the Exeter Diocesan Architectural Society until 1853, an early member was the Revd Samuel Edmund Walker, whose father, an affluent barrister and Master of the Exchequer Office, had purchased the wealthy living of St Columb Major in 1826. Walker, who had been the incumbent at St Columb since 1841, was determined to rebuild his dilapidated, moated rectory, which, before a fire in 1701, had also contained a college of priests and deacons. Reputedly costing about £7,000, White's rebuilding followed the previous plan, with the rooms arranged around an open, central courtyard, but with access to the upper storey provided by a fire-proof stone staircase (Fig. 7). *The Ecclesiologist* believed the design was 'very good indeed; it will look a very model of domestic religious architecture ... [although] too large for the residence of any one priest'.[13]

Despite the insertion of additional windows and the loss of flêches, the building of slatestone rubble with limestone dressings and slate roofs has survived relatively unscathed, the traceried windows reflecting the society's preference for the Middle Pointed, although the transoms reveal that White had not completely abandoned Perpendicular for secular buildings. Colour is restricted to the tracery of the principal windows, where White's typical geometrical stained glass (Fig. 8) contrasts with the pale, clean lines of the granite staircase (Fig. 9). It must be remembered when comparing this building with White's other parsonages, or with those of his contemporaries, that Walker intended it to become the palace for a new bishop of Cornwall. It was in order to increase the value of his endowment of the living of St Columb for the bishopric that Walker invested in property development in Notting Hill. His plans included a church and choir school in memory of his parents, and it was this commission for St Columba's Church, later All Saints', that occasioned White's return to London around 1850.

However, while White was still based in Truro, his eldest brother, the Revd Henry Master White, offered his services to Robert Gray, Bishop of Cape Town since 1847, 'for five years at his own expense', and left England on 27 August 1848.[14] Bishop Gray had found on his arrival 'no system of education for the youth of the upper classes', but in March 1849 he opened a school 'conducted strictly on the principles of the English Church' under the direction of Henry White, in unoccupied buildings adjacent to his residence at Protea (now Bishopscourt), Cape Town.[15] In April 1849 Henry White wrote to William explaining that

> *in the present house there cannot be much increase of numbers, & as more are likely to apply for admission, I think before long some new buildings must be erected, or another house looked out. Now it seems to me that there are very great advantages in buildings erected for the purpose, & therefore I wish you to turn the matter over in your mind so as to be ready to send plans if I write for them – and particularly to see Radley so as to know their system, & the advantages of their internal arrangements. ... What I want is*

to have large bed rooms, with each bed parted off as it is at Radley, as that system allows of more privacy to each boy than anything short of separate bed rooms for each.[16]

The dormitory, with its emphasis on the rule of 'Sileatur in Dormitorio', was of great importance to Radley's co-founder, William Sewell, although his regime provoked criticism from some of the old school who thought it 'calculated to make the boys milk-sops'.[17] However, others believed it was a system 'in many respects better suited for the sons of gentlemen who are wished to be brought up as gentlemen' and advocated 'introducing wooden partitions between the beds, after the fashion of the medieval dormitories, as has been adopted at Radley. This would itself cure some of the worst evils of the old system'.[18] Henry White, having endured 'the roughness and brutality ... of Winchester', obviously agreed.In a letter home dated 9 August 1849, Henry remarked that 'There were two more boys come to the Collegiate School, so that we now have nine. I think it likely, though nothing is yet determined, that by Christmas another house may be procured for us! But we say nothing about it yet.'[19] However, there were many practical difficulties associated with the construction of a new school, as Henry had made clear:

In this country building is very expensive: there is but little building stone, (a short time ago none had been found near here); the country bricks are bad; so almost all houses are plastered or stuccoed. Both masons & carpenters wages are high, especially those of the better sort of workmen ... Good timber is dear, though deal may be got at about English prices ... I wish you would consider what style of building is likely to be cheapest in such a state of things.[20]

Although Henry wanted lofty rooms 'for the sake of coolness', he did 'not wish for any great ornament any where but should like to have the interior of the Chapel well arranged, and fitted'. He promised to enclose a rough sketch of his ideas for a building 'requisite for 40 or 50 boys, leaving space for subsequent additions. Just think over what wd. be the expense of doing it in the plainest way in England; & we may say double that for the Cape.'[21]

By September 1849 Henry was writing to his younger brother (Francis) Gilbert White telling him that

The Bishop has just purchased a house and a piece of ground, (about 50 acres) for a future College ... Woodlands, as the estate just purchased is called, is about 5 miles out of Cape Town, and it is generally considered to be as healthy a situation as any in the District.[22]

Henry also explained that 'Our new dormitory will easily admit of such an arrangement as that at Radley, and by enforcing strict silence there, we may secure to each boy entire freedom and privacy for his Morning and Evening Prayers.'[23]

In November, Henry was again writing to William to ask about metal window frames and quarries, to discuss the problems caused by the shortage of water and to remind William 'that the North is the sunny side.'[24] William must have sent some preliminary plans, for Henry remarked that the main gateway needed the emphasis of a tower 'or something else over it.' Henry acknowledged further plans in April 1851, presumably those referred to by *The Ecclesiologist* as White's 'very admirable' design for a quadrangle comprised of chapel, hall, school-room, covered play area, cloister and accommodation for staff and servants, that had to be abandoned for financial reasons. Although White's subsequent scheme lacked 'any pretence at architectural beauty', it could boast a 'good and suitable outline, and with all the actual requisites for the institution.'[25] These buildings of 1852 survive in Founders Quad (Fig. 10, view from north-west): the east range comprised, on the ground floor, a masters' common room, vice-principal's room, and prefects' study, with the chapel at the southern end; a long dormitory and master's room occupying the first floor. A 'short high wall' (now the area with three close-set dormers) separated this block from the southern range of schoolroom (with tall lancet windows) and lobby, over which was a room used as a classroom and boys' library. Although William did not attend university, his brother's education at Oxford, and Pugin's admiration for the medieval collegiate system based on the quadrangle, were obvious influences, which, through this design, were transported to the Cape.

These early buildings prefigure White's long and prolific practice, which comprised churches, both new and restored, parsonage houses, National Society and public schools and commercial buildings, as well as private houses. White deplored the 'tardy pace' of the Gothic revival in secular architecture, which he blamed on 'much too servile imitations of ancient models'.[26] His later designs demonstrate that he was in the vanguard of the development of Gothic, employing elements of the Queen Anne style well before they were recognised as such, and promoting the use of local materials and vernacular styles that presaged the Arts and Crafts movement.

Fig. 10 | The Founder's Quad, Bishops College, Cape Town, 1849–53: view from the north-west

NOTES

1. Mark Girouard, 'Humewood Castle, Co. Wicklow', *Country Life*, 9 May 1968, p. 1213.
2. Thomas Henry Watson, RIBA *Journal*, 10 February 1900, p. 145.
3. William White, *The Builder*, vol. 49, (1885), p. 623.
4. RIBA *Journal*, 10 February 1900, p. 146.
5. Miss H. M. White's MSS notes, Bishops College archive, Cape Town.
6. *The Ecclesiologist*, n.s. vol. 6, (1849), p. 262.
7. William Haslam, letter, 31 July 1848, ICBS File No. 3905, Lambeth Palace Library.
8. *Royal Cornwall Gazette*, 4 May 1849; W.D. Longlands, letter, 29 March [1849], ICBS File No. 3833, Lambeth Palace Library.
9. William White, letter, 13 April 1849, ICBS File No. 3833, Lambeth Palace Library.
10. *The Ecclesiologist*, n.s. vol. 7, 1850, pp. 246–47.
11. Clive Wainwright, 'Ardent Simplicity', *Country Life*, 18 October 1990, p. 151.
12. [G.H. Fellowes Prynne], Obituary, *Architectural Association Notes*, vol. 15 (1900), p. 20.
13. *The Ecclesiologist*, n.s. vol. 9, (1851), p. 234.
14. H. L. Farrer, *Life of Robert Gray*, London, 1876, p.183; *The Guardian*, 1848, p. 567.
15. Robert Gray, Lord Bishop of Capetown, *Journals of Two Visitations in 1848 and 1850*, London, 1852, pp.223–24.
16. H. M. White to William White, 27 April 1849, Bishops College archive, Cape Town.
17. Anonymous review of *Preface to the Sixth Edition of "Tom Brown's School-Days"*, *Gentleman's Magazine*, Vol.205, 1858, p. 73. I am most grateful to the Archivist at Radley for bringing this to my attention.
18. Ibid., p. 73.
19. Quoted by his daughter, Miss H. M. White, MSS notes, Bishops College archive, Cape Town.
20. H. M. White to William White, 27 April 1849, Bishops College archive, Cape Town.
21. Ibid.
22. H.M. White to F.G. White, letter dated 6 September 1849, reprinted in *South African Church Magazine*, October 1852, pp. 311–17. Gray was provided with the funds to buy the estate by Angela Burdett-Coutts, see John Gardener, *Bishops 150, A History of the Diocesan College, Rondebosch*, Cape Town, 1997, p. 220.
23. H.M. White, *South African Church Magazine*, October 1852, p. 317.
24. H. M. White to William White, 28 November 1849, Bishops College archive, Cape Town.
25. *The Ecclesiologist*, n.s. vol. 10 (1852), p. 301.
26. William White, 'Upon Some of the Causes and Points of Failure in Modern Design', *The Ecclesiologist*, n.s. vol. 9 (1851), p. 307.

ACKNOWLEDGEMENT

I should like to acknowledge my gratitude to the Paul Mellon Centre for the Study of British Art for a generous Research Grant that allowed me to examine White's buildings in South Africa.

Contributors

PAUL BRADLEY completed a PhD on the country houses of William Burn at the University of Nottingham in 2004.

TIMOTHY BRITTAIN-CATLIN is the author of *The English Parsonage in the Early Nineteenth Century* (Spire Books, 2008), which includes the first detailed analysis of A. W. N. Pugin's unusual house plans. An architect, urban planner and for nearly 20 years a regular contributor to *The World of Interiors*, he has taught at the Bezalel Academy of Art and Design, Jerusalem, and the Architectural Association School of Architecture in London. He is today a lecturer at the Kent School of Architecture, University of Kent. In 2008 he also published *Churches*, an introduction to church design and history for the general reader.

JIM CHESHIRE is Senior Lecturer in the History of Art and Design at the Lincoln School of Art and Design, University of Lincoln. He is a specialist in the design and material culture of the nineteenth century. Publications include *Stained Glass and the Victorian Gothic Revival* (Manchester University Press, 2004) and 'Space and the Victorian Ecclesiastical Interior' in Janice Helland and Sandra Alfoldy, eds., *Craft, Space and Interior Design 1855–2005* (Ashgate, 2008). He is currently working on an exhibition about the transformation of Tennyson's poetry into visual culture and editing the associated catalogue, which will be published by Lund Humphries in 2009.

HELEN DUNSTAN-SMITH is the manager at Haslam & Whiteway, Kensington Church Street, London.

CAROL A. HRVOL FLORES is Professor of Architecture at Ball State University. An architecture historian, specialising in the history, theory and criticism of British and American architecture in the eighteenth, nineteenth and twentieth centuries, her publications include award-winning articles on the use of inscriptions in architecture and on American public housing. Her book *Owen Jones: Design, Ornament, Architecture and Theory* (2006) received the Henry-Russell Hitchcock Book Award for 2007 by the Victorian Society in America.

MICHAEL HALL is the editor of *Apollo*. His books include *Waddesdon Manor* (Abrams, 2002) and *Victorian Country Houses* (Aurum, forthcoming 2009). He is chairman of the Victorian Society's events committee and is writing a book on Bodley and Garner.

ROSEMARY HILL's *God's Architect: Pugin and the Building of Romantic Britain* was published in 2007 by Allen Lane. Her most recent book is *Stonehenge*, published in 2008 by Profile. She is a trustee of the Victorian Society, a Fellow of the Society of Antiquaries and a member of the editorial board of *The London Review of Books*.

GILL HUNTER lives with her husband in Reading, Berkshire, a town renowned for its nineteenth-century brickwork. An MA in Victorian Art and Architecture at Royal Holloway College was followed by a PhD at University College London on the work of William White. Dr Hunter was introduced to some White buildings during research for John Elliott and John Pritchard (eds), *George Edmund Street, a Victorian Architecture in Berkshire*. White was remembered as a follower of A.W.N. Pugin, whose own church at Ramsgate was the subject of Libby Horner and Gill Hunter's book for the Pugin Society, *A Flint Seaside Church* (2000). Following some teaching and lecturing, Dr Hunter is now working on a monograph of William White, which it is hoped will be published in 2009.

GAVIN STAMP is an architectural historian and writer. Having taught at the Mackintosh School of Architecture, Glasgow School of Art, for some years, he has now reverted to being an independent scholar. He has written about the architecture of Alexander 'Greek' Thomson, the Gilbert Scott dynasty, Robert Weir Schultz and Edwin Lutyens as well as about London's earliest photographs, the architecture of electricity and telephone boxes. His most recent books are *The Memorial to the Missing of the Somme* and *Britain's Lost Cities*. He has been a member of the Victorian Society since 1966 and has always believed that railways are one of the greatest contributions of the Victorians to civilisation.

Office of Charles Barry, *The New Houses of Parliament: Contract No 3 River front, Bays and Buttresses*, inscribed *Drawing No 95, Contract No 3* and dated *Westminster Jan 13th 1841*, pen and ink and watercolour extensively inscribed, 28½ × 18 inches (detail): see Chapter 5, p. 77

THE VICTORIAN SOCIETY

The Victorian Society is the champion for Victorian and Edwardian buildings in England and Wales. Our aims are:

CONSERVING

To save Victorian and Edwardian buildings or groups of buildings of special architectural merit from needless destruction or disfigurement.

INVOLVING

To awaken public interest in, and appreciation of, the best of Victorian and Edwardian arts, architecture, crafts and design;

EDUCATING

To encourage the study of these and of related social history and to provide advice to owners and public authorities in regard to the preservation and repair of Victorian and Edwardian buildings and the uses to which they can, if necessary, be adapted

The aims are linked, and through involving and educating the public, we can increase the likelihood of conserving buildings.Victorian and Edwardian buildings are irreplaceable, cherished, diverse, beautiful, familiar and part of our everyday life.

They contribute overwhelmingly to the character of places people love and places where people live. They belong to all of us. Their owners are really only custodians for future generations. Victorian and Edwardian buildings are part of our collective memory, and central to how we see ourselves as individuals, communities and as a nation.

When decisions are taken which affect their future, the debate must be open and informed. We need to understand what is special about Victorian and Edwardian buildings and landscapes so that any necessary changes can be incorporated without damaging them forever.

We don't want to lose our past through ignorance.

That's where the Victorian Society comes in. As a reservoir of expertise, as energetic campaigners, and as a community organisation bringing together individuals from all round the country, we have helped people save the buildings they value. Sometimes it has been major national monuments such as the Albert Memorial in London or the Albert Dock in Liverpool, but more often nowadays it is local churches threatened with closure or good houses flattened to make way for undistinguished offices.

1958
2008